WINNING THE BATTLE
FOR THE
MINDS OF MEN

WINNING THE BATTLE
FOR THE
MINDS OF MEN

DENNIS PEACOCKE

ALIVE & FREE
Santa Rosa, California

Published by ALIVE & FREE, 131 Stony Circle, Suite 750
Santa Rosa, California 95401.

Except where otherwise noted, all scripture quotations in this book are taken from the New American Standard Version, © *The Lockman Foundation 1960, 1962, 1963, 1968, 1971, 1972, 1973, 1975, 1977. Used by permission.*

ISBN 0-9618934-0-0

Printed in the Uniited States of America.

DEDICATION

To my family who sacrificially gave me up
once again for the Kingdom;
to Bob and Rush and Gary who helped
re-engage my earlier training; to my uncle
Jim who first caused me to bow my knee to
Jesus, and perhaps most specifically to my
initial tutor — thanks, Mom.

CONTENTS

ACKNOWLEDGMENTS

To so many who helped me birth and develop this project, I am deeply grateful. For Sandy, Rod, Loran and for Gary Metz and his final re-direction—I am blessed by your jobs well done. May this foundation serve us well in the tasks to which we are called.

The worker must one day seize power, in order to erect the new organization of labor; he must push to one side the old politics which uphold the old institutions, if he does not want to suffer the loss of heaven on earth, as did the old Christians who neglected and despised it.

KARL MARX
Address at The Hague Congress (1872)

Dropped Into The Battle Zone

You are involved in a battle to the death between two competing world systems over the control of this planet. At birth you were dropped in the midst of the battle zone. Although most Christians are unaware of the immediacy of this battle, every single one of us is involved because neither one of the two warring "superpowers" will allow any of us to remain neutral. This war is being fought both with ideas and raw power. In our lifetime (or perhaps, by stretching it, in our children's lifetimes), it will erupt into ultimate confrontation.

This is the ultimate battle between God and Satan, between the kingdom of God and the world system, between Jesus Christ and the devil. The battle lines have been drawn, the challenge has been raised and there is no backing out. Though by appearance things may appear to be "normal", the armies nevertheless are amassing as "the kings of the earth [world system] take their stand against the Lord and against His anointed [the Church]".[1] We are moving into the time of the earth's fire.

Freedom's only hope is in God—God working out His plan of the ages through His people, the Church. Christians and Christians alone of all the people in the earth can possess the moral fervency and ideological consistency necessary to mobilize the armies of righteousness to a successful confrontation. They alone possess

---

[1] Psalm 2:2

the moral fuel and the truth that frees.[2] Christians, under the guidance and in the power of the Holy Spirit, are the only visible hope for a world trapped in increasing fear, despair and bondage.

Calling Christian Heroes

This book is a call for Christian heroes, for Christians who will stand up for the faith and pursue righteousness both in their own lives and in society: no matter what the cost.

This book will (1) show clearly the necessity of "occupying (in victory) until Christ comes;"[3] (2) expose ways the enemies of God's moral order are trying to destroy not only our communities but our children's futures; (3) show how you can find your place of service (ministry) in the battle;[4] and (4) teach you biblical principles in understanding and shaping political and economic events.[5] It will also jar you.

Christians cannot afford to look at the world through splintered lenses, mixing and matching Christian principles with the principles of the Opposition. Christians must look, live, and act with an integrated *Christian worldview* to successfully participate in the ultimate victory of the Lord in His work. It is this Christian worldview alone that will allow the Church to cut through the smoke of deception shrouding the battlefield for the minds of men. True Christianity recognizes that God's Word speaks to all that man is and does — and it deals with ultimate issues. True Christianity is looking for a world ordered in such a way that His kingdom comes, and will is done *on earth* as it is in heaven.[6]

Birthpangs, Death, and Strong Men and Women

For nation will rise against nation, and kingdom against kingdom. ..but all these things are merely the beginning of birth pangs (Matthew 24:7, 8).

I'm not preoccupied with "doom and gloom," but I am obsessed with the promised redemption of a fallen world. Jesus spoke of the tumultuous last days as "the beginning of birth pangs." There is pain and suffering to come, but the result is life not death,

[2] John 8:32, 36. [3] Luke 19:13. [4] Ephesians 4:7; I Peter 4:10. [5] Ephesians 3:10. [6] Matthew 6:10

birth and not annihilation. We Christians can, should, and must play out our courageous part in this labor and birth process as the Lord prepares for His return. I am convinced from careful study of the scriptures that we don't have to—in fact should never—give up and let Satan have any uncontested power over the earth. Satan is a bully who rules by fear and deception. Christian liberators must declare the truth: Satan is a defeated enemy, defeated at the cross. Christians have a duty before our Lord and Master to bring both Christ's victory and His message of redemption to liberate the nations. Our message of Christ's kingdom is designed to set men free personally, in their families, communities, nations, and even in the world.

True freedom is measured by the degree to which a culture honors human dignity, recognizing men and women as created in the image of God.[7] Ultimately, to reject God also rejects the value of man. The more truly Christian a culture is, the more it is moral, free, productive, and civilized. Conversely, the less Christian it is, the more poverty, exploitation, hopelessness and death exist. In our own case, as the western world moved into the twentieth century, it cast off the restraints of historical Christian values and substituted Freudian psychology, scientific socialism, and evolutionary relativism, bringing us a century of death. Evolution teaches us that man, as "evolving muck" has no special claim to life, and that all relationships are based on the ethics of the power of the survival of the fittest. An evolving world is based on and legitimizes incredible cruelty. The wide spread acceptance of evolution has given us the most barbaric period in history.

The Century Of Death

Over one hundred and fifty million human beings have been killed in this century (not counting war casualties) at the hands of torturers, through planned famine, by executioners, or by abortionists.[8]

Where was the Church in all of this? Mostly deaf, dumb, and blind—doing nothing more than wringing its hands and waiting for Jesus to come.

[7] Genesis 1:26. [8] Wall Street Journal, July 7, 1986. *War Isn't This Century's Biggest Killer.*

Millions have died in the Soviet Union, Cambodia, Southeast Asia, Red China, Africa, Afghanistan and other countries. Millions have also died in their mothers' wombs. *This is the bloodiest century in history.*[9] These millions upon millions of corpses are mostly the victims of anti-Christian governments and/or ideologies which reject God's moral absolutes. When values become relative, so does the value of human life.

This has been a unique century of ideological warfare on a mass scale. While the religiously misguided of the Inquisition killed their thousands, the *secular humanists, Marxists*, and *abortionists* have killed and continue to kill multiplied millions. These myriad victims die because Christians fail to invalidate the death sentences issued by the world-system upon them. Neither political dissent nor being a fetus that is "inconveniencing" its mother's lifestyle ought to be a crime worthy of death.

Slow death is epidemic also. Sexually-related plagues are incubating a medical holocaust. Drug use is out of control; public "education" has become a misnomer; world debt is swelling to a crushing tide; liberal welfare policies are systematically destroying the black family unit; and criminals are wasting the peace loving at home while Marxists destroy the freedom-loving abroad.

We're Even Losing Ground Evangelistically!

Consider the current dimensions of our evangelistic losses. In the last fifty years, the Moslem religion has increased in size 500%; Hinduism by 117%; Buddhism by 63% and Christianity by a mere 47%. Not only have we lost two thirds of the globe politically since 1917 to the Marxists, but we are currently losing the religious world as well.[10]

The Question: How Did This Disaster Occur?

Don't look elsewhere for the causes of this moral cancer—look to the Church. The nations are in misery and Christian civilization is *perishing* more because of *false doctrine in the Church* than because of universal sin or Satan's power. *The Church*

---

[9] Ibid. [10] *The Church Around The World*, April 1986.

is where God chooses to act and liberate as he "takes His stand."[11] When the Church *withdraws* from society, the institutions within it will decay and increasingly practice inhuman indignities. The nations are perishing because the Church has withdrawn from shaping their laws and influencing their cultures. Christian withdrawal brings decay, collapse and death. But there is no need for this Christian flight from battle: Jesus promised us that "greater is He that is in you than he who is in the world" (1 John 4:4).

Theological deception has led us into withdrawal from society and into a nearly exclusive concern with *internal church life* (privatization). Because nature abhors a vacuum, the secular state has rushed in to fill the vacuum of valueless society. It has set its own godless standards for man, standards of relativistic values and increasing degradation. For too long the Church stood back from the world and decried its ever-increasing slide into the quagmire of decay. But we have not realized that *our withdrawal* from an active role in caring for and discipling our nations is the major cause for this accelerating self-destruction. Our defective theology has shot the nations in the foot.

The Answer

It is time to reverse this disintegration of civilization. It is time to re-assert our God commanded role to be "salt and light and a city set on a hill."[12]

In order for us to be liberators of the nations, and truly disciple them, the Church must reinvolve itself in impacting the whole world socially, politically, and culturally for Christ. We must get involved, like Jesus did. Involvement recognizes that the Church must act and be liberated itself as it turns to the job of discipling the nations.[13] We must allow God to free the Church so we can be a free-flowing conduit of true freedom, from God to all men. The journey to freedom begins with the recognition of your own bondage and your commitment to breaking out of it. Contemporary Christians have allowed themselves to be ghettoized, shoved into a corner where we entertain ourselves and primarily

---

[11]Psalm 82:1; I Corinthians 6:19. [12] Matthew 5:13-16. [13] Matthew 28:18-20

demonstrate our concern for a heavenly future. We have fled from the battlefield on this earth instead of courageously acting to bring God's power to bear in the midst of it.[14]

Strong Men for Strong Times

It's time to break out of the Christian ghetto. It's time for the church to reclaim the agenda for change from the world system. It's time to assert the truth of God over the lies of His enemy. The battle promises to be fierce, because most men, including Christians, have been brainwashed by the world system. We Christians tend to have souls that are saved but worldly minds. Remember however that the King of Glory rides at the head of our army. And He is *already* declared to be "the King of Kings and Lord of Lords" (Revelation 19:16).

Dare to meet the challenge. God is recruiting Christian men and women just like you who can retrain their minds and qualify to carry his righteousness and justice to the imprisoned. May this book teach you how to become vitally relevant as you become the "salt of the earth." May your tombstone read:

"IT MADE A DIFFERENCE THAT THIS SOUL LIVED"

---

[14] Psalm 110:2

He said therefore, "A certain nobleman went into a far country to receive for himself a kingdom, and to return. And he called his ten servants, and delivered them ten pounds, and said unto them, 'Occupy till I come' "
(Luke 19:12,13).

CHAPTER ONE

Occupying Till He Comes

So you want to live a Christian life that really changes people and things? Great. The cry for a relevant church and personal lives that count can only lead us toward the hard work of clear thinking. Clear thinking begins by asking the right questions. Let us begin with some basic questions and a little hard work before we get to the more 'exciting' issues of our journey toward a vibrant church and world-changing Christians.

How did the world get into the mess it's in today? What does our culture's destruction have to do with the Church? What part in this battle for the nations do I play as an individual Christian? How can I find my own ministry? These are the questions I usually get first when I recruit Christians to join Christ's army to liberate their nations. The answers to these questions form the foundation of this book. Lets start with the "basics" of our situation.

Spiritual Law Upholds All Things

There are no human activities in which God is uninterested or uninvolved. Jesus is Lord of all and cares about and is involved with all that exists. But He is *not* the source of the world's problems. Problems have their origin in spiritual disobedience. They are ultimately the result of flaunting and/or improperly applying the laws of God's universe.

1

God created an ordered universe of cause and effect. All mankind functions within its ordered borders—even if some segments of humanity hate God and His laws. Spiritual laws and natural laws are both all-inclusive and inexorable. Gravity was created by God and works whether you believe in it or not. God's laws, whether spiritual or natural, work in the real, here-and-now world.

The Bible is filled with God's laws for man's use in integrating every part of his life to successful spiritual and physical living. The Bible is the 'manufacturer's handbook.' God created the earth, man, and all the laws that govern His creation. Nothing can fall outside of God's spiritual laws. Science, economics, politics and all other aspects of human life work properly only to the degree that they are in obedience to God's laws. Today, society is falling apart because it is increasingly a spiritual criminal as it systematically breaks God's laws.

The World in Rebellion

The world system is in rebellion against God and the Church has largely refused to challenge this rebellion or even to censor it. We have allowed Satan to convince us that the world's problems aren't 'spiritual,' and so they are none of the Church's business. Instead of studying God's word and becoming experts in the knowledge and application of spiritual law in every facet of human life, we have studied only enough to change man's soul but not his world. We have turned God into a 'moralist' instead of seeing Him as a creative ruler. We have let the wicked rob God's store, as it were, being content to simply get a few of the store's customers out safely. We have not resisted evil and attempted to uphold the laws of God before all men. In short, we have failed to disciple the nations because we have not taught them to obey 'whatsoever things I have commanded' in every *realm* of human life.[1]

---

[1] Matthew 28:20

The Church is God's Custodian

When the earth's caretaker, God's Church, goes to sleep on the job, everybody suffers. Every aspect of human society is affected, by our benign neglect. We have the stewardship over God's word and God's word is where healing and health for the nations is found. By and large, Christians have only applied God's word to the Church. We have let the unsaved live by their 'own laws' since we thought the laws of the Book didn't apply outside the Church. The result is an uncared-for world of people, choking in the confusion of their own disobedience. When the Church falls into theological error, the world suffers. Jesus left the Church as His representative, occupying until He returns.[2] If the Church abandons its care and responsibility for the nations, the world becomes like a rental property abandoned by the rental agent, subject to vandalism and destruction. This is exactly our present situation. Because of the false doctrine of withdrawal, the Church has abandoned the nations. The lawn and flower beds are overgrown and vandals have all but destroyed the house. The vandals are those anti-God leaders who have infected the nations with political and social programs totally at odds with the laws of God's universe.

Untying The Custodian

God's word has the answers for all of man's problems. Jesus didn't just say that those in the Church should live by every word from God, but that *man*, meaning every single human being, can only live successfully by God's word.[3] God's word is the door to blessing and liberty. The key to that door into God's blessing has been given to the Church to lead the nations into true freedom.[4] Our problem is that we haven't used those keys to solve the problems that are killing the world.

Matthew 12:29 warns that plunder is only possible when the 'strong man' has been bound: "Or how can anyone enter the strong man's house and carry off his property, unless he first binds the strong man? And then he will plunder his house." Jesus tells us

---

[2] Luke 19:12-15; Matthew 25:14-23. [3] Matthew 4:4. [4] Matthew 16:18, 19

how to steal another's property: bind the strong man. Christ's property is the world, the nations.[5] We, the members of His body, the Church, are the 'strong man' who is to guard and protect Christ's nations. To steal the nations from God, the Church must first be bound. False doctrines of abandonment and deception chained us and made us powerless to stop the decay of the nations. Our enemies didn't have to kill Christianity, they only had to get us to abandon our responsibility for others and give us an obsession with 'pie in the sky' escapism. With us preoccupied with other things, God's enemies can do with the nations what they will.

The Enemy's Chains

The enemy's lies are chameleon-like in their varieties of expression, but the core of each is the same: "give us the real world and you Christians can do what you want with the 'spiritual' future!" "Leave the nations alone," false teaching tells us. "They belong to Satan. Take heaven, and be content. Besides, Jesus said His kingdom 'was not of this world.' He was offered the nations when Satan tempted Him in the wilderness, but He refused. Jesus isn't interested in working through the Church to influence the world. He simply plans to judge it at His second coming.

"Everywhere in scripture the world is described as wicked, evil and to be shunned at all cost. We are to flee from it. The earth belongs to Satan. Involvement in the affairs of this world, especially politics, will corrupt you and distract you from saving souls for the heavenly kingdom. When Christians forsake evangelism and the saving of souls for involvement with the social gospel, they totally miss God."

Do arguments like this sound familiar to you? Can you think of other scriptures that the 'abandonists' can take out of context to prove to you that you should keep your hands off society and the nations? Does it shock you that the most powerful spiritual attacks come from the misuse of scripture? It shouldn't. Reread the temptation of Christ (Matthew 4:1-11). Jesus and Satan banged heads in the wilderness with the correct use of scripture at the

---

[5] Psalm 2:8; 24:1; 82:8; etc.

4

core of their battle. Satan continuously uses scripture against the Christian to keep him convinced that 'real world' problems are not the church's business.

Freedom in God's Word

Since the earth is to burn[6], does that mean Christians should leave the care of it and its nations to the enemy? No. Never! Christians are told to disciple and care for the nations by teaching them to obey God's laws and prosper.[7] We should have the same care and concern for our transitory earth as we do for our corruptible bodies. Our bodies will decompose when we die, but we haven't stopped eating, sleeping, bathing, clothing and caring for ourselves, have we? Then why should we abandon the care of our Father's earth?

In Genesis, man was told what God expected him to do with his time on earth. "Be fruitful and multiply, and fill the earth, and subdue it and rule..." (Genesis 1:26-28). This command has never changed. Jesus came to set His people free from the power of sin so that they could obey that ancient law of God.[8]

God's goal for man is to bring us into obedience through the atonement of Jesus Christ so that God and man can be reconciled and work together. *God wants us to rule under Him over the world.* God has called a people for Himself to co-rule as His companion.[9] God never saved His people for an eternity of sitting on clouds, wearing golden slippers, and playing harps. He saved us for leadership in His kingdom, both here on earth and in the age to come.[10] For Christians, the future is now. We are *already* in His kingdom training program.[11] Each of us who has been cleansed by his blood has entered the royal apprenticeship, and we are to 'reign in this life.'[12]

Disobedience Leads To Dispossession

The Bible starts with the identification of God as the absolute Creator.[13] He created the earth and He is its original and only

---

[6] II Peter 3:10. [7] Matthew 28:19. [8] Romans 8:2-4. [9] Ephesians 1:17, 18. [10] Romans 8:17; Hebrews 2:5. [11] Colossians 1:13. [12] Romans 5:17 KJV. [13] Genesis 1:1.

owner.[14] God still owns absolutely everything on earth, including the nations.[15]

Adam and Eve were made in God's image.[16] Adam was God's first-born earthly son, the lawful heir to the whole world. God made it for man, and then He placed man over it.[17] All of it. It was man's lawful possession, so long as man remained faithful to God.

But Adam walked away from his communion with God by succumbing to Satan's false promise that he would not die by disobeying God, that, in fact, he would be on the same level as God because he would "know good and evil" (Genesis 3:5). Adam chose to believe Satan's lie over God's command.

People are still imitating Adam's sin today. Secular humanism shoves Christianity out of the public arena as it declares, "We're all like God. We can each decide our own morality, our own ethics and laws, our own destinies. Everything we need is within ourselves. We don't need God and we certainly don't need you uptight Christians."

God's response to Adam was immediate and clear. He drove Adam and Eve out of the Garden of Eden, disinheriting them from His riches.[18] From that day on they were legally disinherited children. So is every human being at birth. We are still created in God's image, but that image has been marred and we are born as disinherited children.

Through Adam we have chosen to reject God's authority and so lose His inheritance and His authority. It is through fallen human beings that Satan seeks to rule the world. He hasn't enough power by himself. Mankind is still mankind, made in God's image. Dominion is still God's assignment to man, not to Satan. God's assignment to man to exercise dominion across the face of the earth is still in force. There is no reason for God's redeemed people to allow Satan any authority at all. Satan and his demons scare men, tempt men, and confuse men, but they cannot rule God's earth beyond men's consent. Satan is lord, not over God's earth, but over the corrupted worldly system his human followers

---

[14] Psalm 24:1. [15] Psalm 2:8;8:28;Genesis 14:19; Deuteronomy 10:14; Exodus 19:5; etc.; [16] Genesis 1:26; [17] Genesis 1:28. [18] Genesis 3:23,24

have constructed. Christians' unbelief gives Satan his power over the nations.

Obedience Leads to Possession

God wants Christians today to bring order to the earth on His behalf. Jesus' words are very clear in Matthew 28:18-20: *"All authority has been given to Me in heaven and on earth; go therefore and make disciples of all nations...teaching them to observe all that I commanded you."*

As the last Adam, Jesus took back the title to the earth after His glorious resurrection. The title deed to the nations is a blood-stained document which Christ took in His possession at the cross. He "spoiled principalities and powers" and made an open spectacle of them (Colossians 2:10, 15). Satan is the god of the corrupt world system, but he certainly doesn't own the earth, or the earth's proclaimed trustee, the Church.

Jesus has all power on the earth, and all power over nations—now! And it is through the Church that he will exercise that power. Satan, unredeemed persons, and all ungodly forces of hell want you to stay ignorant of this all-important truth. The Church is "political" whether you like it or not, because it is God's source for governmental wisdom and law for the nations of His earth. The Church is the "pillar and ground of truth" (1 Timothy 3:15), and it alone has the keys which will unlock the nations. Jesus gave us the keys. We are compelled to use them!

The Church Is Not...

If we are to occupy until He comes and care for His goods, then we must understand how God sees the Church and how He expects it to *represent His interests* on the earth. We must see the Church as God sees it, as the representative of Himself and guardian of the Master's property.

The Church is not a building. Most Christians recognize the snare of identifying the people of God with brick and wood, but we can still play into the hands of our enemies if we identify ourselves too strongly with a particular location—where we hold our public assemblies. We "ghettoize" ourselves if we do, shutting ourselves out of the surrounding cares of our society. If we can be tricked into identifying the people of God and their purposes with simply going into a building, instead of seeing God's people as spiritual agents working on God's behalf on the earth, then we buy into the mentality of "ghetto Christianity."

The Church is not a meeting. Many people have stopped seeing the Church as a building only to be snared into believing that the purpose of the Church is to have one meeting after another. It is very easy to fall into this trap, since the fellowship of the saints is vital to spiritual health, and our assemblies are where we worship, and learn. But, as essential as meetings are, the Church is not a meeting.

The Church: God's Vessel To Serve The Nations

The Church is not a building of stone, but we are a temple of "living stones" (1 Peter 2:9). We are not a series of meetings, we are a place where God meets. We are the place where "God takes His stand" (Psalm 82:1).

This means that God has no other group of people on the earth through whom He operates freely. God wants to deal with injustice through the Church. God wants to aid the poor through the Church. God wants to help the fatherless through the Church. God has decided that any degree of divine control on the earth before Christ's return will come through the Church. That is where He "takes His stand."

The Church is to be a beacon of light to the nations as it challenges them to come out of the darkness. The light of the Church should be so bright and so compelling that the nations will trade in their chains and rags for the freedom and robes of righteousness from Christ. The light of the Church should shine into every nook and cranny of human captivity and imprisonment. Evangelism should be a natural outgrowth of every Christian's natural interaction with people around him. It should never be relegated to a "special program" status which hides it from instant access by the needy.

8

The Church must break free from false doctrine and false ideas about itself. It must recognize that God's master plan is for responsible leadership of our society, not for the satanic lie of the isolated Christian ghetto. Most church members are set on *leaving* the planet and its problems as quickly as they can get to heaven. But God has set His heart *toward* the people of the earth and the furtherance of His kingdom here on this planet as the *Church's first duty*. God wants to rule through us. While we have been driving to free ourselves of the earth and its problems, God has been pressing toward the earth and the care of its people. Let's go God's way—toward the needs of the people and the care of His planet! Let's occupy our post and not desert it.

...if you love me,...tend my sheep

(John 21:17)

CHAPTER TWO

The Care and Discipling
of God's Nations

So the Church is supposed "to occupy till He comes"—what does that mean? It's certainly more than just holding bigger and bigger meetings until the Second Coming. The occupying that the Bible talks about is active, not passive. The Church is the strongman God has left as His steward on the earth until the return of His Son. As stewards, we have commitments and responsibilities which God expects us to fulfill as His agents. Our faithfulness in carrying out these responsibilities reflects our understanding of God's love for the nations.

God's Love for the Nations

God's love for the nations is stated and implied throughout the entire Bible, from Genesis to Revelation. His love is expressed through His authority and righteous judgment over the nations.[1] In Genesis we see Abraham, our "father of the faith" (Romans 4:16), declared the father of many nations as well as many believers:

> *Abraham will surely become a great and mighty nation and in him all the nations of the earth will be blessed (Genesis 18:18).*

In the book of Revelation, God's unending commitment to the welfare of the nations continues on into eternity with these tender words:

---

[1] Psalm 82:8

And he showed me a river of the water of life, clear as crystal, coming from the throne of God and of the Lamb,...on either side of the river was the tree of life, bearing twelve kinds of fruit, yielding fruit every month; and the leaves of the tree were for the healing of the nations (Revelation 22:1-2).

"The nations" does not mean "a big collection of people." God cares about individuals, in fact He "purchased" them with the blood of His Son,[2] but He also cares about social units (families, communities, governments, nations). God loves the nations, and the closer we Christians come to His heart, the more we feel His anguish over them and the more we can open our hearts to His commission of working on behalf of their liberation.

The Nations as Christ's Inheritance

The destiny of the nations is at the heart of Christ's future plans. His post-resurrection commission to His disciples was to wait in Jerusalem until they had received power from the Holy Spirit.[3] *Why* were they to receive God's power? Was it to be spent on themselves in their own private church meetings? Was it simply to speak in tongues or to enjoy church meetings? No! They received God's power for the same reason you and I receive it—to bring salvation to the lost and healing and liberation to the nations.[4]

In Psalms 2:8 we are told that the nations of the earth have been given by the Father to our Lord as His possession: "Ask of Me, and I will surely give the nations as Thine inheritance, and the very ends of the earth as Thy possession."

As Christ's joint heirs,[5] the nations therefore have become the stewardship of His bride, the Church. They are ours because they are His. If we love Jesus, we will honor His commitment to His Father to care for the Father's gift to Jesus.

The nations really do belong to God and He wants them back from the satanic system that has enslaved them. Christian involvement in the political issues of the nations becomes the shepherd's rod by which Christians guide the wayward nations home to their

---

[2] Acts 20:28. [3] Acts 1:4,5. [4] Acts 1:8. [5] Romans 8:17

Creator and Shepherd. As we stand for God's Word and press for the application of His principles in all areas of society, we prod the nations along. God is reluctant to use tribulation, poverty, and anguish to get them to turn their hearts toward home, but use them He does when the church's pastoral care for the nations proves ineffective. Our neglect helps bring down God's judgment upon them. Christ-centered involvement in the affairs of the nations is the most powerful way to call an *entire population* to Christ. It puts the issues of the gospel in the newspaper, in the voting booth, on television, in the daily conversations of even unbelievers. Citizens of the kingdom are commanded to press all men for social, economic, and political obedience to biblical principles. When we do, then all people, wherever they are in society, will have to deal with the claims of Jesus Christ—not because they go to church, but because they cannot escape His word as the pervasive conversation topic of a new way to structure their nation. We are taking God's word to them instead of asking them to come to our meeting!

Finding the Nations' Destiny

All nations whom thou hast made shall come and worship before thee, O Lord (Psalm 86:9).

Nations, like people, have purposes and destinies for which God has created them. The Church's job as the Father's earthly steward and discipler for His nations not only is to lead individuals to their personal destiny (salvation), but also to lead whole nations to their destiny (national redemption). The nations are vehicles of God's cosmic plan:

He made from one man every nation of mankind to live on all the face of the earth, having determined their appointed times, and the boundaries of their habitation, that they should seek God, if perhaps they might grope for Him and find Him, though He is not far from each one of us (Acts 17:26,27).

God's Design for the Nations

God wants both individuals and nations to obey Him so that they will prosper in every way and fulfill their unique purposes in God's overall plans. Sin is not simply 'doing the wrong thing.' It actually creates a barrier between people and God's blessing for them. It keeps them separated from their destiny. Through repentance and discipling, nations as well as individuals are led into spiritual and earthly clarity as to why they are created. In this sense a true patriot is one who loves his nation and hungers to see it fulfill God's purposes for it. This pattern of Godly admonition and instruction to equip men and nations in fulfilling their destiny is found throughout the scriptures in the following pattern:

1. The standard of conduct God requires from us.
2. The blessing and creative life we will experience if we obey His standard (our destiny).
3. The poverty and death we will experience if we disobey God and walk in our own self-determined law.

Obedience to God's laws lead men and nations to their destinies and ultimate place of service. When they disobey they are derailed. When they are obedient, the evidence of blessing clearly *reinforces* their chosen compliance with God's word. In other words, the Bible is designed by God to be a self-evident thermometer that registers health or danger in *this world* as men measure their lives against what God promises them as rewards or penalties for obeying His laws. You really can 'keep score' to some degree before you die.

For example, Israel was promised, among other things, that a nation obeying God's moral laws could expect a positive balance of payments and world leadership position in international trade and finance markets.[6] It was also promised that disobedience to God's law would produce a nation of debt, dependency and slavery to foreign nations.[7] God's word is filled with this form of encouragement and admonition for individuals, families, churches, businesses, and even whole nations.

---

[6] Deuteronomy 15:6; 28:12-13. [7] Deuteronomy 28:25, 29, 43, 44

The Church's job is to serve as a doctor to the nations, diagnosing their health needs as we read their vital signs against the chart of health or disease God lays out in his word. If they are sick, we should know why and what to do about it.

God's Care for His Created World

For God so loved the world that He gave His only begotten Son that whosoever should believe in Him should not perish but have eternal life (John 3:16).

The world order that God has created for man to tend and steward, and for which Jesus died, is called the "kosmos" in the original Greek of the New Testament. *Kosmos* has interesting origins which reflect God's benevolent care for the inhabited world. The word comes from *komeo*, which means "to tend for, care for, and bring order to." This meaning is consistent with God's original "dominion mandate" for man outlined in Genesis 1:26-28. Man is told there that he is to hold the earth in covenant with God, applying God's laws to it so that it will fulfill his purposes and flourish. The world has been marred by thousands and thousands of years of sin and death, but God has given Christians the tools—the Word of God and the personal gift of the Holy Spirit—to take dominion.[8]

Obedience to God's laws unlocks more than individual blessings for those who have been saved by grace. Obedience also unlocks God's blessings for the kosmos.[9] Jesus' death on the cross paid the penalties of disobedience, and the blessings promised both for individuals and nations from God's Word are available through the power and administration of the Holy Spirit.

The "good news" that Christians bring for the nations is liberation, not bondage to religious tyranny. Think of the wider implications of the Church's favorite verse, "For God so loved the world, that he gave His only begotten Son, that whoever believes in Him should not perish, but have eternal life" (John 3:16). Of course God's love encompasses the "whoever," the individual. But this verse states clearly that God loves the created world (kosmos)! Christ's sacrifice also procured the liberation of the

---

[8] John 14:16. [9] Romans 8:21-23

nations, so that His treasuries are now theirs! This is incredibly good news! God's love for His creation goes beyond simply loving man and Christ's resurrection releases that love to the entire created order. He really does love the created world enough to give Jesus to release it!

How Do We Disciple A Nation?

There will be no end to the increase of His government or of peace on the throne of David and over his kingdom. To establish it and to uphold it with justice and righteousness from then on and forevermore. The zeal of the Lord of Hosts will accomplish this (Isaiah 9:7).

As we now know, Christians are commissioned to care for and disciple the nations. Caring for them means to bring them God's peace and God's peace comes from His *government.* There can be no peace without godly government as Isaiah tells us. Government *precedes* peace. When Christ came to earth, the process of extending his peace to his world began. The Scripture says that God's government is ceaseless and all-pervasive. The Church's job is to let God establish Christ's government to the nations through it. So, discipling nations intimately involves the process of discovering how the *government of God functions through men.*

How can the Church even begin to tackle the worldwide task of caring for the nations? Where do we start?

God doesn't ask us to tackle everything at once. God doesn't ask us to produce a completed canvas without first teaching us and then enabling us to paint it section by section.

God has broken down man's kosmos order into more manageable units for *governing.* There are five natural *governing units,* or spheres, to the kosmos that comprise the kingdom of God's government. All government falls into one or another of these five categories:

1. The individual (Self-government)[10]

---

[10] Proverbs 16:32; 25:28; Luke 9:23; Acts 24:25; I Corinthians 9:25; II Corinthians 10:5; Galatians 5:22-24; II Timothy 1:7; Hebrews 12:11; II Peter 2:9-19.

2. The family (Family government)[11]
3. The local church (Church government)[12]
4. The commercial (Economic government)[13]
5 The civil government (Civil government)[14]

God's Word has set standards for governing each one of these units or spheres, and each one is blessed through obedience to those standards or suffers through disobedience. God holds man responsible to govern each of these five spheres of human activity according to God's directions for it and expects the harmonious result to give God a good return on His investment.[15] In other words, God doesn't simply want order on the earth, He wants increasing blessing.

God is organized and orderly, governing through these systems. We must teach people and nations what God requires from them personally in their families, in the churches, in their economic stewardship, and finally in their civil institutions. The instruction of the *whole man* becomes the totality of the commission Jesus gave His Church.[16] We cannot neglect any one of the five governing spheres without disobeying the Lord's Great Commission. To disciple a nation is to teach its citizens to fully obey and reach their potential in each one of the five spheres. A nation of such people is a nation under God's government and will experience His peace.

The kingdom or government of God is not simply goose bumps or angels' wings or exciting experiences. It is God's ordained *order* functioning harmoniously *between* the five spheres, the Holy Spirit maintaining the ecological balance of power with the attendant blessings of wholeness and peace.[17]

Tyranny and Balance

The Word of God provides the only hope for the proper management of *power* among these five governing spheres. The world

---

[11] Genesis 2:18; 3:16; Deuteronomy 6:1-9; Ephesians 5:21-31; Colossians 3:18 [12] Matthew 18:18-20; 22:21; I Timothy 3:1-15; 5:17-22; Titus 1:6-9; I Thessalonians 5:17; Hebrews 13:7,17; I Peter 5:1-5; [13] Exodus 20:15-17; Numbers 27:1-9; Deuteronomy 8:17-18; 28:1-18; Proverbs 6:1-5; 10:2; 11:4; 13:22; 15:16; 23:4-5; Philippians 4:19; Hebrews 7:4-10; I Corinthians 9:6. [14] Exodus 18:19-23; Deuteronomy 1:13-17; II Samuel 23:3-4; Psalm 2:10-12; 33:12; Proverbs 8:12-16; 11:11; 14:34; 29:12; Isaiah 10:1; Romans 13:1-7; I Timothy 1:8-10. [15] Luke 19:21-23. [16] Matthew 28:18-20. [17] Romans 14:17

system is not only in rebellion against God, it is in rebellion against the balanced operation of these five units of government designed by God to bring order to his kosmos. The Church is supposed to teach the nations how to find the proper use of power and government. This is *how* the Church should bring correction to injustice within a nation and lead it into God's desired order.

Let's look at a diagram that helps explain this truth:

The Five Spheres of Human Government

GOD'S THRONE
(Psalm 89:4)

Justice and Righteousness
↓
CHRIST

The Sphere of
SELF GOVERNMENT

The Sphere of
FAMILY GOVERNMENT

The Sphere of
CHURCH GOVERNMENT[18]

The Sphere of
COMMERCIAL/ECONOMIC
GOVERNMENT

The Sphere of
CIVIL GOVERNMENT

Notice that the Church is at the center of this diagram, Christ is over the Church, and God's throne of justice and righteousness presides.[19] The Church is to be the priestly, teaching, and prophetic voice to the world. Its responsibility is to correctly interpret the Word of God to all the forms of government. Its job is to hold that Word up to all other institutions, including itself, as a plumbline for human conduct.

---

[18] 1 PRIEST (Teacher-healer, on God's behalf). 2 PROPHET (Guardian of God's vision and investment). [19] Psalm 89:14

The New Testament teaches us:

All Scripture is inspired by God, and is profitable for teaching, for reproof, for correction, for training in righteousness; that the man of God may be adequate, equipped for every good work (2 Timothy 3:16,17).

"All scripture" means just that, all scripture. Not just personal salvation passages. Not just rapture passages. Not just the New Testament. This "all scripture" means the whole Bible, Old and New Testaments, and passages for the structuring of the social order as well as for the healing of individuals. Please remember, the New Testament was not even fully written when Paul referred to the power of God's Word. The believers of Paul's day thought the "scriptures" simply meant the Old Testament!

Separation of Power

A Christian philosophy of government in each of these five spheres consists of the ability to make sure that power is properly held and balanced proportionately for each governing institution. The Bible provides us with these guidelines.

Tyranny is not some black figure out of the night, leaping into the midst of society. Tyranny is abuse of power. Tyranny results from the improper accumulation of power in one institution or sphere. The whole of modern culture is moving deeper and deeper into tyranny under the misguided principle of centralization. The anti-God forces are continually transferring more and more power to civil government, in effect castrating our individual freedom, our families, our churches, and our economy. The centralization of power into the state is the most dangerous trend in the world today.

The first sentence of Rousseau's *Social Contract* is a living reality today, over two hundred years after it was first written (1762): "Man is born free; and everywhere he is in chains." Although man may be born without a consciousness of slavery, the Bible tells us that man is born a slave to sin. Nevertheless, Rousseau is right that men everywhere are in chains. If man is ever to be free, he must exchange sin's chains for Christ's freedom—freedom

21

in all spheres of life. Freedom can only reign when Christ reigns in all things.[20] Each of the five governing units God has ordained—the individual, the family, the Church, the economic/commercial realm, and the civil government—must subordinate itself to the purposes of Christ, finding their perimeters of authority and responsibility in His government alone.

The War With Tyranny

If Christ is not reigning, then either the individual, the family, the Church, the commercial realm, or the state will rise up as a false point of human focus. Men will always deify one or another aspect of the creation. Carnal man cannot avoid worshipping the created rather than the Creator.[21] Even the Church, strange as it seems, can be exalted to tyrannical power in a Christian's life, becoming out of balance with both the Lord and the other institutions of human society.

The State as God

In our contemporary world, it is civil government, the State, that has reared its head in an ungodly attempt to replace Christ as the *centering agent* of all human life. The state, in modern political theory, increasingly demands that the individual, the family, the commercial realm, and the Church bow down before it, and give it first place as a "god." The opponents of Christianity claim that the state is "the will of the people." Instead, the state subverts individual will to collective tyranny.

The state demanded first allegiance in Christ's day too. The war then was between Christ and Caesar. It has all come full circle. However, to the early Church's credit, it took barely 300 years for Christ to triumph over Caesar through his Church. Our legacy from our Christian brethren is a legacy of *victory* over tyranny, not defeat by tyrants. But victory requires Christian *faith* and *involvement* and this is what must be restored in the Church today.

When the state starts talking about its being "the voice of the

---

[20] Colossians 1:15-18. [21] Romans 1:18-23

people," watch out! Some bureaucrat or politician is about to pass a law or administrative order that will fleece your pockets, restrict your personal property or take your life. The state is not God, try as it will to hold all authority because it calls itself "the voice of the people."

The state as tyrant sublimates all rival spheres by regulating individual belief and thought, family size, structure, and authority; crushing free religious assembly and expression, controlling all aspects of the economy, and assuming all ultimate power for itself.

The Individual as God

A fool does not delight in understanding, but only in revealing his own mind (Proverbs 18:2).

When our lives center on personal pleasure and convenience and when our life goal is to discover every nook and cranny of our own wonderful little selves, tyranny emerges. Preoccupation with "self" will turn everybody and everything else into *objects* whose only worth is in their ability to satisfy our selfish urges. People are dehumanized when they become objects, becoming victims of exploitation, expendable refuse. Whatever is not valued because of its unique creation by God is dismissed through an act of evolutionary arrogance. The Marxists and decadent West are equally able to turn humans into "things."

Unborn babies are called "tissue;" women are called sex-objects; sex is self-gratifying and divorced from love; children are exploited emotionally and physically for their use as personal stimulants; minorities become second class citizens and "the enemy." In the world of self-actualization and self-centered universes, self is "God" and the law of this "God" is exploitation, personal "rights," and exploitation of others.

The Family as God

When the family usurps Christ as the center, it produces a tribalism or clannishness that prevents man from cooperating in larger units. The possibility of unity beyond the family is impaired. If the family is not balanced, no other social institution

can survive. The kingdom of God is weakened and distorted when
the family becomes tyrannical. Individual family members look
to their own natural families as the circumference of their involvement in life, abandoning the divine plan for his natural family
to *fit harmoniously with the other institutions of the kingdom.*
The classic teaching of Jesus on this point is:

> *...and someone said to Him, "Behold, Your mother and*
> *Your brothers are standing outside to speak to You."*
> *But He answered the one who was telling Him and said,*
> *"Who is My mother and who are My brothers?"*
> *And stretching out His hand toward His disciples, He said,*
> *"Behold, My mother and My brothers!*
> *"For whoever shall do the will of My Father who is in*
> *heaven, he is My brother and sister and mother"* (Mat-
> thew 12:47-50).

The family is our home base, but important as it is, it is not
the ultimate unit. Christ alone is.

The Local Church as God

Can the local church become a tyrant? Yes. Any institution ordained by God can become tyrannical when it claims that it is
the most powerful and deserves the obedience of all the others.
The individual must answer to God,[22] the family must answer
to God,[23] the local church must answer to God,[24] the commercial realm must answer to God,[25] and the nations must answer
to God.[26] All must bow their knees to *Him* alone.[27] Christ's government brings peace because it balances all claims to ultimate
authority.

When the local church assumes the throne which belongs properly to Jesus Christ, members sacrifice their individual relationships with Christ to the corporate life of the church. Church
families lose their unique natural unity and are splintered into
fragments floating in the sea of church activities and commitments,. Responsible social and economic activism is
sublimated to the limited and shortsighted needs of the local

---

[22] II Corinthians 5:10. [23] Joshua 7:24-25. [24] Revelation 2:4-5. [25] Deuteronomy 14:22. [26] Psalm 72:11.
[27] Philippians 2:10-11.

24

church. Competing commitment to the other four spheres is seen as intrusive and disruptive, the local church becomes "a law unto itself." Tyranny on the local church level is a hollow mockery of the true purposes of the Church in God's order.

The Marketplace as God

For what does it profit a man to gain the whole world, and forfeit his soul? (Mark 8:36).

When the commercial sphere becomes the center of life, it produces ruthless exploitation of man by man and self-indulgent materialism.

Capitalism, in a biblical context, is the promotion of individuals using private ownership to produce increase. The Bible stands unequivocally behind the right of the individual to private property and his attendant responsibility to be a good steward, to bring and share increase.

But what happens when the commercial issues become our "god?" Employees are not loyal to their employers: they're only loyal to money and benefits. Employers are not loyal to their employees: they're only loyal to hefty profit margins. Unions go to any lengths to amass wealth for the workers, and corporate tyrants exploit their employees in the race for the almighty dollar. Corporations don't work for the good of society, they work for the good of their balance sheets. Personnel don't give their best, they give the minimum required by law. Tenure and unionization has often produced sloppy work and unbridled free enterprise has cruelly exploited the workers.

Those who worship the state tell us that the solution to commercial exploitation is for the state to appropriate the means of production, extending the tyranny of the state into yet another realm. Even well-intentioned Christians are drawn into this false philosophy through the guise of "liberation theology," which replaces Christ with economic "justice" (obtained through violent revolution). It falls into the reverse trap of exploitive commercialism; instead of exploiting man for economic reasons, it cuts off man's ability to be a creator through developing his own private property.

25

False Gods of Failure

When the individual rises up to be the center we have anarchy; when the family rises up to be the center we have feudalism; when the Church tries to take Christ's place we have religious tyranny; when the marketplace attempts to supplant Christ, we have mutant, ruthless capitalism; and when the state tries to take Christ's place, we have deadly authoritarianism.

True biblical pluralism, that elusive balance between differing institutions and responsibilities, is possible only when Christ is the center of all things, and every other human institution is held in proper balance. It is this balance that the Church is to practice and multiply in the world around us.

God's Word is the Church's most precious possession, for in it is life. It alone tells us how to view God, ourselves, the ordering of all life, and final reality. It is relative to nothing, unchanging, understandable and accurate. It is the glasses through which the Church must view all things (a Christian world view). Handling the Word of God properly is the Church's ultimate stewardship from which springs the nations' only hope. If we do not give them God's *whole* Word for the nations' *whole* life, we give them only a portion of Christ—not enough to free them. All men are required to live by it (Matthew 4:4), all men will be judged by it,[28] and all social laws should be set by its standards.[29]

Pride of Ownership

Everyone who has ever owned a business knows the difference between the attitude of an employee and the attitude of a proprietor. The proprietor cares about everything from the cleaning of the floors to the filing of the tax forms. The employee stops at quitting time and tends to view only his own job. The owner is concerned with the entire endeavor while the employee can't see beyond his own self-interests.

Our Father is calling for a generation of believers to emerge in His Church who dare to become proprietors in attitude with Him.[30] He hungers for us to water and teach and prune and care

[28] Romans 1:20, 2:12-15. [29] Matthew 28:19. [30] Romans 8:17, Galatians 4:7

26

for His vines. Stewards, everything the nations do is our concern; they are part of our Father's business. Let's stop being employees and accept our responsibilities as heirs! Let's disciple nations by teaching them what God requires of both *individuals* and the four other spheres of God's earthly government that surround them.

And those from among you will rebuild the ancient ruins;
you will raise up the age-old foundations; and you will
be called the repairer of the breach, the restorer of the
streets in which to dwell

(Isaiah 58:12)

CHAPTER THREE

Reclaiming The Power of
The Early Church

Starting with a small, rag-tag group of men and women, the early Church brought the world's mightiest civilization to its religious knees as Christianity and its gospel conquered Rome within three centuries.

If the early Church had thought that it was to withdraw from the surrounding culture, like we have, it never could have done this. Rulers don't run and runners don't rule! I am eternally grateful that the early Church *did not* interpret the gospel of the kingdom the way much of the Church does today. Had it done so, human history would have been infinitely darker.

How do you test someone's belief? Do you listen to what they say, or watch what they do? Everyone would agree that people's actions preach their convictions far louder and more persuasively than their words. If we are to rediscover the foundations of power within the Christian gospel, as the living example of a gospel that *actually did* liberate nations, we must examine the early Church's actions. Their actions tell us what obeying the Great Commission to "disciple nations" actually meant to them. They were 20 centuries closer to Jesus than we are, and their score for "nations freed" far outstrips our own.

Putting the Counterfeit System Under Our Foot

One thing we know about those early nation liberators for sure— their message touched more than simply men's souls, It grabbed the counterfeit system of Satan's world order and crushed its head.[1] The early Christians turned the world upside down:

> *And when they did not find them, they began dragging Jason and some brethren before the city authorities, shouting, "These men who have upset the world have come here also; and Jason has welcomed them, and they all act contrary to the decrees of Caesar, saying that there is another king, Jesus* (Acts 17:6, 7).

There is another king than Caesar! This king is the "King of kings," economic orders, churches, families and individuals. He is the Lord of Glory, our Great God and Savior, Jesus Christ.[2]

What is the gospel? What is the counterfeit world order Satan has set up by which he imprisons the nations and opposes Christ's gospel? How did the early Church interpret the "battle for the nations"? These questions will be answered in this chapter.

What is the Gospel?

All cultures need "moral fuel" in order to command the respect of their citizens. God has made all men religious. The only issue is, will man turn to Christ's religion or to his own? This "God-shaped vacuum," as some call it, must be filled with somebody's gospel. All men are religious, even if the god they choose to worship is the self or the power of the state. Somebody's gospel is running or trying to run the ship.

Any gospel (the true one or an imitation) is built on three components:

1. The alleged *facts* of the gospel
2. The *purpose* these facts lead us to
3. The *spirit* in which the gospel is implemented

When Jesus said that His kingdom was not of the world system's order,[3] He was saying that His view of the facts, purpose, and spirit of reality were totally at odds with the gospel of this false world order. The battle for the nations is a battle between two gospels.

---

[1] Genesis 3:15. [2] Titus 2:13. [3] John 18:36

The Facts of Our Gospel

Christians should agree with the following seven facts of the Christian gospel:

1. *Creation.* God reveals Himself as a creator and worker who seeks fellowship with his created beings as He assigns them work on His behalf.[4]
2. *Dominion.* God places man on the earth to fill the earth with His purposes for it.[5]
3. *Salvation.* Man has fallen into sin by choice and, because God loves man, God has provided a savior—Jesus Christ—to save man from his sin and permit him access to God and the blessings of obedient relationship with Him.
4. *Incarnation.* God became flesh in Christ, died for our sins, rose the third day—according to the Scriptures—and, having spoiled the powers of Satan set against Him at the cross, has ascended into heaven as the Lord of the universe with all power.
5. *Judgment.* Christ will physically return to the earth to judge all men for their responses to His truth and then consummate, with His Church, the complete reign of God on His earth through his kingdom.
6. *Revelation.* God has revealed His perfect will for all men through the special revelation of his word—the Bible—and displays His presence and laws in the orderly world of His creation.
7. *Responsibility.* All men are to respond to God's call for obedience from them, to order their affairs according to His laws and principles, and to accept God's power to please His as they grow into the work and maturity which God ordains for them.

The Purpose of Our Gospel

What are you and I called to do with these facts? What is the purpose of this Christian gospel? I believe the answer is simple: to assert this gospel in the earth and challenge, with all conviction, those systems of thought and action that resist Christ's gospel.

[4] Genesis 1-3. [5] Genesis 1:26-28, Numbers 14:21, Psalm 46:10

If it is a true gospel, an ultimate gospel, and a gospel by which all men and nations shall be judged, then it is a gospel that forces those who truly believe it to boldly assert it both inwardly and to whole cultures. It is a gospel by which all systems of contrary thought, both individually and nationally, must be exposed and undermined.

For though we walk in the flesh, we do not war according to the flesh, for the weapons of our warfare are not of the flesh, but divinely powerful for the destruction of fortresses. We are destroying speculations and every lofty thing raised up against the knowledge of God, and we are taking every thought captive to the obedience of Christ (2 Corinthians 10:3-5).

The Spirit of Our Gospel

The spirit in which this gospel is preached must be a spirit with a sense of final authority. God's Word is not in error, the world is in error. We need not apologize to the world for pulling the sheet off its nakedness. We need only to offer it healing and answers that work. We are to challenge to the death all that enslaves man and impoverishes him, leaving him hollow and sterile. We are to convince him that sin is more an obstacle to creativity and blessing than simply refusing to obey an arbitrary God. God loves man enough to invite him into His work as a junior partner.

We need to be militant in our assault against the sham walls that imprison the nations, and yet tender with the prisoners themselves, who find our speech a threat to the familiar routines of prison life. We must attack the ideas, not the men. The battle for the earth is won or lost in the way men think and through the gospels the rulers impose upon the masses.[6] Ours is a gospel of militant truth and serving love.

The World-System: A Gospel of Exploitation

Satan also has a gospel. It takes many forms but its essential

---

[6] 2 Corinthians 10:3-5

core is this: Christ's gospel is incomplete. Satan's system, which the Bible also calls "the world," is run by Satan[7] and is set up as a false world order contrary to how God wants to rule his kosmos. Satan does not own either the earth or God's kosmos; he only wants the Church to believe that he does, so that it will not challenge his rulership or assert Christ's. Please note that Satan's power is directed at men's view of reality. To the degree he controls the mind, he controls all other political systems:

The god of this world has blinded the minds of the unbelieving that they might not see the light of the gospel of the glory of Christ, who is the image of God (2 Corinthians 4:4).

Satan's world order is only as powerful as the coils of deception that bind our minds. Free the Church, and the ensuing final contest will pit against each other the full forces of heaven and hell on earth. Be of good courage. I have read the last pages of the Bible and we win!

The satanic order is made up of three basic sub-systems. The foundation is *invisible*, but very real, and supports the visible systems operating on the earth. Satan has intertwined the three because he knows that God's Word says that "a three-fold cord is not easily broken" (Ecclesiastes 4:12), and he always copies God's structures—they work. Satan's world order is founded with demonic principalities and powers set up over national borders[7] and run by a satanic chain of command.[8] Upon this invisible foundation he has raised two *visible* bondage systems: (1) false religious systems, and (2) false political-economic orders.

Its Demonic Foundations

God's invisible order supports His visible Church, and Satan's invisible authorities support his earthly puppets. In order to assault the satanic world order, we must first pray against its spiritual foundations. Liberators who attack the visible political or religious order without first using our 16" prayer guns to soften its demonic foundations are doomed to defeat. In the battle for the nations, prayer isn't something "spiritual," it is necessary for survival!

---

[7] 2 Corinthians 4:4. [8] Daniel 10:13. [9] Ephesians 6:12

The demonic forces upholding Satan's interests are organized on the basis of controlling particular national borders. Satan's kingdom is set up along the lines of the *nations* in imitation of God's plan, because God orders the affairs of men through the nations.[10] Therefore, effective prayer in this battle must be directed especially against the particular demonic structures ruling over particular nations.

The Counterfeit Political-Economic Order

Satan's counterfeit political-economic order is machinery designed to further tyrannical corruption. In most places today, money from economic leaders puts the leaders in power in political structures by influencing the voters. Remember the imitation "golden rule?" Those who have the gold make the rules! The political leaders, bought by the economic leaders, then select the judicial leaders. The power of the judges allows them to interpret how the laws of the system will operate. In particular, they set the rules for how the economic orders will work.

Money sets leaders in power, who in turn select the legal interpreters, who in turn set the rules as to how the money merchants can operate. It's tidy and it comes down to money and resources. It is not intrinsically evil, but it becomes evil because economic gain sets the standards rather than God's laws.

God's Political Order For Nations

Before we resume our study of Satan's world system, I must insert here a few quick comments on how God's political order for the nations is designed.

As already seen God's government is to function through harmony and obedience to the principles of the five spheres of government. Separated but interrelated powers is God's governing model. A society aligned to God's kingdom in the civil sphere is structured like this:

God's Law Order (The Scriptures)

   1. Determines the principles of the national constitution

---

[10] Acts 17:26

2. Determines qualification for leadership
3. Determines qualifications for individual voting rights
4. Enforces godly law

In this system all men are equal under God's law and equally responsible to it. This system is essentially the foundation upon which the United States civil government was established, today's corruption notwithstanding.

Satan's Religious Bondage System

Let's return now to our analysis of how the world system is structured. The religious systems of man are built on one of two equally false assumptions about reality: (1) The affairs of this world are of no value to God since He is "spiritual" and only cares about individual spiritual perfection (all *self-actualizing systems),* or (2) Man is basically good and can attain his destiny by restructuring his *environment.* If he is properly educated and trained, in his own power, he can work his way to wholeness, salvation (secular humanism). All religious systems constructed by man can be categorized generally into one of these two false views of reality. Examples of some self-actualizing systems include Buddhism, Confucianism, Rosicrucianism, and Spiritualism. The branches of Secular Humanism embracing environmental "salvation" include: Marxism/Socialism, Rationalism, and Evolutionism.

Christianity by Contrast

Christianity affirms that man must be personally redeemed by God's power, and that his political environment is to be structured by God's laws. God *does care* about the political environment in which man's personal destiny is worked out. Islam, unlike Christianity, believes that obedience to God's personal and social laws is possible by man's *own power* without the need of a savior (Jesus) or power source (Holy Spirit).

All societies are "religious," even the anti-God ones. Why? Because "religion" is the value system men use to construct the laws that run their lives. Religion is a view of reality by which laws are established that reward some behavior and penalize other behavior. All law is religious because it affirms a moral code for men. (More on this in Chapter Five.)

Religion In Culture

All religious systems have two basic functions in a political/economic order: (1) to legitimize the current political order (or they risk self-annihilation); and (2) to supply the moral fuel that legitimizes the values and stated goals of the culture.

The religious fuel of the secular humanists is man's freedom from God's law through social engineering (socialism) or exalting personal freedom to the point of an absolute right (decadent capitalism). Put another way, men's religions are in league with the political/economic orders they support. They have "sold out" to them and are generally permitted only to the degree they support the civil governments.

The false religious systems of Satan's counterfeit world order are called a "whore" in the Bible.[11] They have rented themselves to the political order's corruption. True Christianity, on the other hand, is called Christ's bride.[12] It *does not sell itself* to justify the corrupt political orders of the world system, but rather rebukes them, exhorts them, challenges them, and teaches them to bring their laws and economic orders into conformity to Christ's commands.[13] The battle for the nations will increasingly begin a "religious" war between the whore and the bride. In the process Christians will be forced by God and the issues of the day to say "good-bye" to polite Christianity. Cultural counterfeit Christianity wants to "win friends and influence people," refusing to challenge the ungodly Caesar and the systems he rules over. God is not a cultural counterfeit Christian.

The Church Is God's Political Validator

How can we as Christians in America begin applying these ideas? Simple. Christians can easily control the swing vote in the United States. Since they are the largest group comprising

---

[11] Revelation 17:1. [12] Ephesians 5:25-27, Revelation 21:9. [13] Matthew 28:20.

about one fifth of the population, they can determine who wins and who loses elections. They must use this power to "anoint" those politicians who announce their support of biblical law or at least the requirements of biblical law in key areas (abortion, inflation, taxation, family, poverty, etc.). Voting is a Christian's priestly function in the civil sphere.

It is the role and responsibility of the Church, as the world's priest to legitimize and bear witness to the power that any law or institution deserves. As God's priest to the nations, the Church is commissioned to both anoint and challenge individuals and institutions to operate *only* within their God-given spheres and under God's laws. Remember, God's kosmos order is established through the five limited spheres of power.

As western societies grow increasingly unstable because of their disobedience, their rejection of the Church, and their resultant depravity, they will experience more and more rebellion from their own citizens. The institution that is disobedient to God can expect disobedience from within itself.

In summary, Satan's world system opposes God's world system (the kingdom of God) and attacks it on three levels: (1) By false religious powers that sell themselves to (2) False political/economic systems that are undergirded by (3) Satan's fallen spirit forces that attempt to hold national populations subject to rebellion, delusion and moral insanity. God is equipping you and me to bring that world order down. As we close this chapter, let's see if what I am saying is what the early church believed as it confronted the world system.

Is This The Early Church's Gospel?

Have you ever played the game where you tell a story to one person, who in turn tells it to another, and another, until it goes around the room and is retold by the last person? It is great fun to hear how the story has changed and become distorted. The point is this. If this battle for the nations is some weird theology or story, we will not find it in scripture or in the early Church.

In Acts 3, we read that Peter and John were on their way to the temple to worship. A poor crippled beggar asked for money, but Peter prayed for the man and he was healed. The religious system exploded, and in collusion with the secular authorities, punished Peter and John, only releasing them because of public threats, back into the care of their fellow Christians.

The evangelicals of today tend to interpret these events only in the context of the power of Christ's witness to evangelize. The pentecostals see the events as a testimony of God's healing power in the Holy Spirit. But how did these early believers who were *actually there* put these events into the context of the gospel as they understood it? Let's read the text:

> *And when they heard this, they lifted their voices to God with one accord and said, "O Lord, it is Thou who didst make the heaven and the earth and the sea, and all that is in them, who by the Holy Spirit, through the mouth of our father David Thy servant, didst say, "Why did the Gentiles rage, and the peoples devise futile things? The kings of the earth took their stand, and the rulers were gathered together against the Lord, and against His Christ." For truly in this city there were gathered together against Thy holy servant Jesus, whom Thou didst anoint, both Herod and Pontius Pilate, along with the Gentiles and the peoples of Israel, to do whatever Thy hand and Thy purpose predestined to occur* (Acts 4:24-28).

God's Healing Power

What an amazing view of the events that early Church had! They interpreted the events surrounding the healing in this way:
1. God owns the earth, not Satan (verse 24).
2. What the supernatural healing pointed to is a battle for the nations prophesied by King David in Psalms 2 (verse 25).
3. That battle in Psalm 2 is characterized as a battle over the ownership of the nations and over the laws that Christ's anointed (the Church) are restraining the rebellious nations with. God wants the kings of the earth (political order) and the judges (law interpreters) to yield to Christ, lest he destroy

them. This is political warfare over the establishment of law!
No other interpretation of Psalm 2 is possible and the Holy
Spirit so records the early Christians' interpretation.

4. In verse 27, they affirm that this healing is consistent with
and affirms Christ's own battle with the world system:
Christ vs. "Herod and Pontius Pilate" (political rulers)
Christ vs. "the Gentiles" (nation systems)
Christ vs. "people of Israel" (religious systems)

God's power and God's people are challenging the entirety of
the world systems' laws, social and religious structures! When
the gospel of the kingdom is preached, it doesn't just address
souls or personal morals; it challenges the whole order of man.
It demands his freedom so that he can serve his God. It presents
the ultimate challenge to the false ruler of man's systems. This
is how the early Church interpreted and lived the gospel.

Riot or Revival

A church that is preaching the kingdom of God and being "salt
and light" is either causing an upheaval or a revival in the fabric
of the nation. (At the very least, it is undergoing persecution.[14])

By this standard, most churches are not currently proclaiming
the kingdom's true message. If they were, they would be doing
now what the Church did in its beginning:

> *And when they did not find them, they began dragging Jason
> and some brethren before the city authorities, shouting,
> "These men who have upset the world have come here also"*
> (Acts 17:6).

The gospel of the kingdom of God attacks the gates of hell[77]
and frees its captives. I used to read the book of Acts as one great
miracle after another. Now I see it also as a series of riotous con-
frontations with the world system, interspersed and fueled by
supernatural power. As a result, the entire three-fold cord of the
world system challenges to the death the Church's hope of occupying and stewarding the nations.

Count on it—the conflict between humanist-based politics and

---

[14] 2 Timothy 3:12.

Christian-based politics is just now emerging. It will escalate and become a battle for the freedom of all nations. The enemy has put the nations of God's earth into his prisons of death and deceit, and the liberators are drawing up in battle formation! In rediscovering the early Church's battle with the whole of the world system, that army of liberators will rediscover the early Church's full power. When the church confronts the world system with the full gospel of the kingdom of God, the full power of the gospel will operate in today's Church just like it did in the Book of Acts.

The execution of justice is joy for the righteous, but is terror to the workers of iniquity

(Proverbs 21:15)

CHAPTER FOUR

The False Separation
of Church and State

The highest form of deception is to get your enemy to destroy himself with ideas you have planted in his mind so subtly that he believes they are his own. The current debate over the so-called "separation of church and state" is perhaps our most dangerous example of such deception. It is an argument framed by the world's political system, erroneously reinforced by the worldly religious philosophers, and, of course, undergirded by the invisible spirits of Satan. It is designed to do one thing: ghettoize Christians, keeping them away from the real issues of discipling the nations. The Church can let the world system control mankind without a fight only if it wants to betray its Leader and condemn to earthly slavery those He died to free.

Dualism Weakens Christians and Imprisons Nations

We discussed two basic categories of the world religious system in the last chapter. One category holds that man's destiny will come out of social restructuring (Humanism, Marxism, etc.). The other holds that, because God is a spirit or a form of higher consciousness, He is unconcerned with matter or earthly political issues.

It is this second false religious concept that has most severely deceived many God-loving Christians. This false view alleges that God is unconcerned with the real world issues of economics and politics. This is actually an Eastern mystical concept, not a Christian idea at all. Unfortunately, over the last hundred and fifty years, this Eastern mystical heresy has entered much of evangelical thought. When the Church falls into false doctrine that pulls it away from the real world issues of man, nations go into imprisonment.

Many Christians seem to think God only wants souls; that He has little use for the bodies in which those souls live. The Deceiver has persuaded the Church to buy into the old religious heresy of "dualism"—a gnostic heresy dismissed by the early Church fathers during the fourth and fifth centuries.

Gnostic dualism teaches that the world and all matter is useless, if not evil and/or illusory. "God wants spirits," it says, not bodies and the work earthly bodies can do to bring God's kingdom to the earth. Politics is seen as "worldly" to a Christian since it deals with earthly affairs. The only work of value for the Christian dualist is preparing people's spirits for heaven. Our beloved brethren, who pass up God's work for us on the earth, have been tricked away from their duty to God to rule over the earth. If matter were evil or useless, Jesus never would have incarnated Himself in a human body. He would have saved man in the form of a spirit.

Religion Is Not Just a Personal Issue

This false eastern philosophy of dualism underpins the erroneous concept of the separation of "church and state" because it gives force to the argument that religion is a personal spiritual issue which must be separated from the real world affairs of government. If you think as a Christian dualist, you really don't care how righteous or unrighteous men's social orders become. The dualist is afraid that the evil world of politics will corrupt the religious purity of our spirit. For him, keeping the Church away from the affairs of state is an obvious religious duty rather than a net of deception, woven to ensnare Christ's nations. The dualist is unable to relate to why Christ wants to assume political power on earth. The following scripture makes little sense to him in the here-and-now world:

> *The kingdom of the world has become the kingdom of our Lord and of His Christ and He will reign forever* (Revelation 11:15).

Separating Fact From Fiction

Let's examine some of the effects of the Church's dualism in today's political thought.

"The United States Constitution guarantees the separation of church and state. Everybody knows that," says the Deceiver. "The wise founding fathers wanted to make sure that they had created a free society where no one's religious convictions would be pushed off on anyone else. In order to do this, the Constitution was written to provide freedom for all religions to operate privately, and guarantees that no religion is allowed to influence or control the political world or the civil government." So argues our "reasonable" foe.

Those who have imprisoned the nations tell us that religion must be kept out of public debates, since religion belongs only in the Church, where its freedom is properly guaranteed. This dualistic doctrine of "the separation of church and state" is written also into the Soviet Union's constitution, Mexico's, and most thoroughly secularized nations.

The more the nations listen to this creed of keeping religion out of the nation's schools and politics, the more society falls apart, the more anarchy reigns, the more murders and rapes and suicides take place.

Do you think the phrase "the separation of church and state" is found in the United States Constitution? If you answered "yes," you are 100% wrong! The Constitution never uses the phrase, "separation of church and state." The Constitution's first amendment simply says that Congress shall make no law establishing a national religion and neither shall it prohibit religion.

A Figment Of Imagination

You couldn't have found "the separation of church and state" in any state constitution back in 1789 either. All the states were openly Christian (except for Rhode Island), and most of them had state-financed churches.

In fact, you couldn't have found it anywhere in 1789 except in the writings of a group of French radical philosophers. In 1794 followers of these French philosophers were chopping off people's heads, especially priests' heads, by the tens of thousands in France in the name of "freedom." America was introduced to the phrase by Thomas Jefferson, a closet Unitarian who had in his desk his own version of the Bible, with all the supernatural passages removed. It wasn't a very big Bible.

Jefferson used the phrase in a letter written to a group of Baptist pastors in Danbury, Connecticut in 1802. The purpose of the letter was to assure those Baptist pastors that Jefferson's somewhat unorthodox view of Christianity would not be pressed on the Church in the United States during his presidency.

President Jefferson assured them that there is a wall of separation that supposedly protects the Church from any undue meddling by the state. The irony is that the phrase never implied that the *state* needed to be protected from the *Church!* Jefferson was guaranteeing the *Church* the benefit of the wall.

The contemporary anti-Christian religious establishment has turned the issue completely on its head by redefining the phrase. This trick is called "historical revisionism." Historical revisionism twists history and interprets it for one's own purposes.

Our Founding Fathers
Consider some of the following quotes from our founding fathers, who wrote, influenced, and/or lived by the wisdom of the Constitution and ruled our nation:

George Washington
It is impossible to rightly govern the world without God and the Bible.

John Adams
Our constitution was made only for a moral and religious people...so great is my veneration of the Bible that the earlier my children begin to read, the more confident will

*be my hope that they will prove useful citizens in their coun-
try and respectful members of society.*
Thomas Jefferson
*The Bible is the cornerstone of liberty....students' perusal
of the sacred volume will make us better citizens, better
fathers, and better husbands.*
Andrew Jackson
*That Book (the Bible) is the rock on which our Republic
rests.*
Benjamin Franklin
*A nation of well-informed men who have been taught to
know the price of the rights which God has given them cannot be enslaved.*
William Penn
*If we will not be governed by God, then we will be ruled
by tyrants.*
Ulysses S. Grant
*Hold fast to the Bible as the sheet anchor of your liberties;
write its precepts in your hearts and practice them in your
lives. To the influence of this Book we are indebted for all
the progress made in true civilization and to this we must
look as our guide in the future. "Righteousness exalteth
a nation, but sin is a reproach to any people."*

The nation's founders knew better than to pay attention to the
dualist's lies about politics and its relationship to religion. The
founders of this nation were wise enough to establish neither a
state church nor make the state non-religious in its value base.
Even the Supreme Court's historical findings support this view.

The Supreme Court ruled in 1799 that "by our form of government, the Christian religion is the established religion." In 1892,
the United States Supreme Court in the case The Church Of The
Holy Trinity vs. United States, examined hundreds of state constitutions, court cases, and other historical documents and reached
the following conclusion:

*There is a universal language pervading them all, having
one meaning: they affirm and reaffirm that this is a religious
nation. These are not individual sayings, declarations of*

49

*private individuals: they are organic utterances: they speak
the language of the entire people....These and many other
matters which might be noticed, add a volume of unofficial
declarations to the mass of organic utterances that this is
a Christian nation* (Supreme Court Case: v. The Holy Trinity, Cited: Feb 29, 1892).

Can the Wall Crush the Church?

The Baptists to whom Jefferson was writing feared state
established churches, and feared political pressures that come with
state established churches. They resented having to pay taxes to
support rival churches. Their fear was rival churches, not rival
religions. They were not living in a Muslim society. They were
living in Christian America. Jefferson promised the church that
the wall would shelter them from any growing incursions from
the state.

However, the wall today does not fulfill Jefferson's design for
it. For example, local cities tax church property to support the
public school system. Since the public school system establishes
our nation's values, it has become the state church, maintained
with taxpayers' money and defended by the American Civil Liberties Union (ACLU).

For over 100 years secular humanists have sold Christians on
the lie that the state is to be protected from Christianity. Now
that the state is huge, now that it takes four to five times God's
tithe of 10%, it has flexed its muscles and begun to wage public
war on the Church.

Rewriting History and Redefining Words

The world system has spent billions of our tax dollars through
public education to convince us of its view of reality, even rewriting
history and redefining words. It spends billions more reinforc-
ing these views through books, movies, magazines, and TV shows.
It has dedicated itself to capturing the media, while Christians
were content to live in cultural shadows.

If you have a child in public school, ask to see his American
history book. See how it deals with the religious history of Christianity in America. Look very hard. You will find almost nothing,

and yet there is absolutely no doubt that Christianity has been the single most dominant cultural force in this nation's history until the early 1900's.

Major religious movements that affected secular history are never even mentioned! The nations are kept in prison through the false words and false history which is their daily diet.[1] For example, the great revival of 1835-45 did more to spur the Civil War on behalf of justice for the blacks than any other social force. The abolitionists came directly out of this revival in the Northeastern states. It was Christians who pressed the issue of slavery to the wall and who broke with other Christians who refused to reject slavery. No self-respecting American historian can deny with intellectual integrity the impact of the revival on the Civil War. But search in vain for its analysis in public school books.

We are told that "to speak of religion in a public text book would be a violation of separation of church and state." Will the Pilgrims next disappear from our history books? Will the Deceiver's duped minions, the ACLU, have the United States' founding fathers as closet homosexuals who, in fact, hated the Bible and left Europe to escape religion in any form?

Religion is Not Just a Private Matter

Over the last one hundred years, the Church has "cut a deal" with western society which was never set to paper or ever openly discussed. In fact it was not understood then, nor is it clearly understood today. The deal was this: Christians would stay out of the political world of governing and setting laws for society, and in return the state would permit the Church to evangelize freely about the future condition of men's souls.

Much of the Church increasingly backed out of political involvements because it felt guilty for a job very poorly done. Until the time of the Reformation in the 1500's, the Church had been integrally involved in the running of society and was guilty both of frequent corruption and tyranny. The Church's role in the political realm was out of balance and it had degenerated into carnal and wicked power plays. Even the unbelievers were

---

[1] Isaiah 5:13

disgusted. Instead of producing kingdom citizens who would bring God's honor and balance to the world's institutional order, it had produced many church leaders who wanted the Church to wield the sword and control all thought.

Martin Luther's ideas became more widely understood and the Church gradually withdrew from the political realm. It became carnal for Christians to be involved in the political process. "Politics is a dirty business," became the affirmation of the Church. We are told to stick to the business of saving souls. The worldly politicians and the devil loved that "deal." It left them a clear field from which to take God's earth unopposed by God's first line of defense, the Church.

Gradually, dualist thinking became the unwritten rule of Western culture: the unbelievers run the world, and the Christians order the private consciences and afterlife of their followers.

But Jesus never retreated from real life, and He challenges us not to. You cannot "Go into all the world" in order to bring it under Christ's obedience if you are lost in your narrow concern with your own soul.

Never Again

We must adopt the rallying cry of the Jews: "Never again!" For the Jews, that cry means that they will never again permit a slaughter such as happened in Nazi Germany. "Never again" carries with it the affirmation that life cannot and will not be taken without a fight. We, too, must affirm that we can no longer stay off the battlefield for God's earth and his nations. Never again will we play religious pattycake outside the political arena while the unbelievers take care of the important job of running God's earth. Never again will we allow the nations of the earth to go down into the depths of human degradation and slaughter without a battle to the end.

The Deal Discriminates Against Conservative Christians

The hypocrisy of the world system is maddening. They not only condemn conservative Christians to the private ghettos between their ears, they are also incredibly two-faced. Humanistic politions do not think it is wrong when left-wing pastors march in support of various anti-American causes. That is considered "Christian duty." But let more evangelical elements of the Church speak, and those same liberal forces cry bloody murder.

The Rev. Jesse Jackson can run for President and not a word is spoken about its propriety, but when Jerry Falwell or Pat Robertson hazards an opinion on anything that the liberals do not like, you would think they had desecrated the flag! Whatever our problems, we have every bit as much right in the political arena as the Berrigan brothers, Bishop Tutu, or Jesse Jackson.

In redefining the "separation of church and state" liberals have temporarily gained some ground, but in the long run they have only created a much more militant kind of conservative Christian activist. The following diagram should help us understand the "deal" more clearly:

Philosophy of the Deal		
"Religion" or what the church should care about.	**The Wall**	**What Belongs** to the world system.
1. Heaven		1. Earth
2. Future		2. Present
3. Men's Souls		3. Men's minds, bodies and time
4. Spiritual Values		4. Real Life
5. Sunday Morning 10 am to 12 noon		5. Everything except Sunday morning
6. Private Morals		6. Public Law and Policy
7. Theology		7. Philosophy, economics, science, business, and anything else that matters
8. Private Conscience		8. Control over God's Nations

WINNING THE BATTLE

"The Deal"

The Spiritual		The Real World
The Individual		Commerce
The Family		Civil Government
The Church		

Welcome to "the Deal." It's such a deal — the world system gets the mine and the church gets the shaft! The "wall of separation" is designed to disembowel the church by cutting off its ability to shape or challenge the money, legal and power structures that run things.

The Lie: Christian Activism Will Destroy Peace and Enshrine Bigotry

In an increasingly godless society, tolerance becomes the supreme virtue and defined religious conviction becomes the supreme sin. The criminal becomes anyone whose standards are tied to God's standards. The "good citizen" becomes anyone who accepts the morality of the lowest common denominator. Excellence dies under the world system's all-tolerating hand.

Our opponents claim that active Christianity in the public sector will lead to enormous social upheaval and unrest. It wasn't the Church that started World Wars I and II, the Korean and Vietnam wars. It was the "enlightened" non-religious nations. Attacks on the Church's responsibility for civil death and the disruption of society tend to be incredibly one-sided and unbalanced. The non-religious have caused multiplied millions more deaths and destruction than did misguided Christians—even during the Inquisition! The Church's dirty laundry is hardly worth an historical footnote in contrast to the more than 150 million plus deaths that the "reasonable and non-religious society" has brought upon us all in the twentieth century. The Christians have killed their thousands, but it takes a secular humanist to kill millions.

54

Religion and Division

But the world system guardians protest: religion in politics will divide the country and lead to disruption of the democratic process." Do they have in mind divisions in society like the ones *they* have already given us—divisions such as labor and management, war and peace, blacks and whites, the old and the young, males and females, and a dozen other hard-core disruptions brought upon the world by those who reject Christianity altogether? Humanists lie about history so much it defies the imagination. Humanistic "concern" for "religion disrupting the culture" is about as wicked as its own unspeakable record of human suffering.

Secular humanism wants raw power and Christians pose a threat to its ugly intentions. Secular humanism dehumanizes people into objects, whether as the victims of abortion, pornographic exploitation, or starvation of those who are "enemies of the non-religious state" (such as in Russia, Southeast Asia, and Ethiopia). What humanism hates most about the Church waking up is that it will unmask their anti-human exploitation and take their foot off people's throats.

I've been behind the Iron Curtain and seen firsthand what a totally non-religious society looks like in its quest for the separation of church and state. One single word describes the sad eyes of its citizens and their colorless clothes and buildings. That word is DESPAIR. And now American humanists want to bring the "blessings" to America of a totally secular society.

Whether the sales pitch for secularism comes from the decadent West, with its sweet insistence that the individual is the center of the universe and that all problems will be solved with more money and time spent on self-actualizing and navel-gazing, or from the Soviets with their "kill the individualist so that all individuals can be truly free," the logic of humanism is fatally flawed. The liberators offer a third choice: the kingdom of God.

Christianity is humanism's great enemy, and the fact that humanists can recognize this reality is the only evidence I have that they can think at all! In their insane desire to separate the spiritual from the real world, they would condemn us all to a society of amoral barbarism. Their "wall of separation" between church and state is, in reality, not a wall but a coffin. But the liberators are going to dismantle this wall. Our love for people compels us to do so.

Who will stand up for me against evildoers? Who will take his stand for me against those who do wickedness?
(Psalm 94:16)

CHAPTER FIVE

Somebody is Legislating Morality

Satan's minion chant the lie that no one (least of all the Church) should "legislate morality" for anyone else. They say the Church has no business telling anybody how to live or what ethical system to obey. Acceptance of this lie stops Christian activism in its tracks, and enshrines wickedness and injustice as the permanent chains of the nations.

Even the Secularists Legislate Morality

All laws tell people what they should do or what they should not do. "Should's" and "should not's" are ethical considerations. And ethical considerations structure every aspect of one's life. The ethical framework within which one lives is one's religion. Laws legislate morality religiously. Public law embodies the religion of any particular nation.

Laws tell men how they will be permitted to live in public (and all too often in private). Laws tell a society what is good and what is bad. This is inescapably a *religious function*.

All societies have laws, and in order to obtain the peace and prosperity of all men, these laws ought to be based on truth that is unchanging. A society that ignores Christ's laws, and opposes his commandments, cuts its own throat and guarantees its own destruction. Laws outside of Christ are organized death.

One of the best explanations of this is given by noted theologian R. J. Rushdoony:

Every law order is a religious establishment; the important question is, of which religion? There can be a separation of church and state, but a separation of religion and the state is impossible. Every law order is simply a moral order enacted. Law says that certain things are forbidden and it establishes penalties for infractions and procedures of enforcement, trial and appeal. Every law is founded on a concept of moral order. The basis of that law in the U.S. has historically been, until recently, a common law Christianity.[1]

Non-Christians want us out of the political arena because they want to live lawlessly (apart from God's laws). This means that they want to make up their own laws as they go along, as if they were God. This is exactly what our heavenly Father does not want men to do. He is asking you and me to establish only those laws that will bring order and justice to an otherwise insane world.

Economist and social analyst Gary North has brilliantly stated the issue:

It is never a question of "law vs. no law"; it is always a question of which law.[2]

God establishes the monopoly of civil government to suppress evildoers.[3] Because it is a monopoly, as the Church is, the magistrate (law-enforcer) is operating as a minister of God.[4] He operates directly under God as a designated agent who bears lawfully delegated authority. But he holds this authority only as God's agent. If he violates God's law, his authority eventually is removed from him and given to another, just as the kingdom of God was removed from the Jews and given to the Gentiles.[5] The only possible basis for maintaining long term political authority is to legislate God's morality, rather than some other god's morality.

---

[1] Rousas J. Rushdoony, *Towards A Theology of Politics, IMPRIMIS*, Vol. 2 No. 2, February 1973, *Hillsdale College, MI.* [2] Gary North, *Unconditional Surrender, God's Program for Victory,* p. 68. Tyler, TX: Geneva Press, 1981. [3] Romans 13:3. [4] Romans 13:3. [5] Matthew 21:43.

Secularists Legislate Their Own Morality

Whoever sets the civil laws rules the nation, and that is why Christ has told Christians in the Great Commission to be the ones who set them. If I say this so many times it's because I need to counteract the 10,000 times you probably have heard that the Great Commission has to do only with evangelism, and not with Christian politics or law.

Opponents of Christianity ask us incredulously, "How can you legislate morality?" What they are really saying is that they want us to live under their counterfeit morality, but they don't want to live under ours. Ours is dependent on a God who judges all men for eternity. Secularists don't want to be reminded of final judgment or their eternal condition without salvation. They have enjoyed legislating their own imitation of morality for the last forty years, and they don't want to quit now. Let's look at some examples of their folly.

Consenting Adult Sin Maims and Kills

Modern secular humanists believe that man creates his own laws for life, independent of any outside direction. They have created a political order that is based on a huge lie that tells us we function independently of each other, *that one's individual sin has no effect on anyone else*–as long as it is done by that ubiquitous non-entity, the "consenting adult." Don't succumb to this lie! There is no such thing as independent sin! All sin, "public" or "private," affects the people as a whole.

The state isn't all powerful or all seeing. But God does see, and He brings judgment. The idea that some sin is private is a lie. The state judges only public evil, or private evil that can be proven from evidence available in public, but no sin is ultimately private.

Private Sin Touches Us All

The concept of private/public is another way of looking at politics. Simply stated, the private/public view of the political order says this: There is no action that I can take in my private life that does not have an effect on all other members of my society. The Old Testament story of Achan at Ai[6] is the classic example of this principle. One man's private sin destroyed his own family and brought defeat on the rest of Israel.

The management of society—which is politics—can only operate successfully from the point of view that society is an extended family of man. What one person does in private has an effect on every other "family" member of the society. AIDS is a shocking and deadly example of this principle. Like ostriches with heads in sand, the humanists nevertheless reject both the family as the basis of political decision making, and also as the link between private and public sin.

The followers of those who have imprisoned the nations actually go into a rage when the liberators say that biblical laws and principles are vastly superior to their wicked laws:

> *Why are the nations in an uproar, and the peoples devising a vain thing? The kings of the earth take their stand, and the rulers take counsel together against the Lord and against His anointed: "Let us tear their fetters apart, and cast away their cords from us!"* (Psalm 2:1-3).

Law is our compass for godly living, and when the law is perverted, it leads only to poverty, disease, and the loss of human freedom.

Man Fails to Find Freedom in His Own Laws

You cannot break God's laws; they break you. Man has been trying earnestly to destroy "superstitious religious" laws in earnest for the last few centuries. Indeed, some misapplied laws have been crippling and destructive, betraying by their fruit their source in *man's* "religious" laws[7] rather than in *God's* laws of life. Modern man finds that the further he gets away from biblical principles, the more ensnared and imprisoned he becomes. Man has abandoned God's laws in pursuit of a freedom he will never find in his own laws.

---

[6] Joshua 7. [7] Matthew 15:6.

Sexual Freedom Is a Lie

The world system is increasingly rejecting monogamy, the limiting of sexual expression to married persons of the opposite sex. So-called "enlightened" human freedom favors human-centered laws that say "anything goes" in the realm of sexual expression. The Deceiver says that biblical law is sexually repressive and based only on man's projected fears. That too is a deadly lie.

Sexual disease is rampant. Even non-Christian medical experts talk about sexually active persons committing "suicide by sex" in today's polluted disease base. In the United States there are 22 million cases of incurable Herpes II, a chlamydia epidemic that is spreading at medically unprecedented speeds, new forms of syphilis and gonorrhea that are resistant to any drug therapy and are now deemed incurable.

Teen pregnancy rates have skyrocketed. Fifty-five percent of black children are born out of wedlock. Millions of babies have died in the last decade from teenage abortions.

The effect of "free sex" on marriage? A 50% divorce rate! (Not all caused directly by sexual degeneracy, but all impacted by it.)

Pornography, sexual violence, and rape are rampant. The 1985 income on pornography in the United States was an estimated $8 billion. Child porn? 1984 estimated income: $500 million. How about 30,000 estimated missing children in the U.S. annually? Rape increases? Try and find a single day they are not reported in your local newspaper. And less than one half of all rapes are even reported!

Let's consider the following nauseating reality given to us by the "morality" of the secularists.

On Justice In America

A survey of more than 300,000 criminal cases, released in April of this year by the Federal Bureau of Justice Statistics, shows that more than half the convicted murderers releas-ed from state prisons in 1983 had served fewer than seven years behind bars. Half the rapists released had served fewer than four years in jail. The median time served by all offenders in state prisons was 19 months. The median term on a life sentence was eight years and seven months. And only 18 percent of those sentenced to life imprisonment served three years before being released. [8]

On Life For Our Teenagers

Every 31 seconds a teenager becomes pregnant.
Roughly every two minutes a teenager gives birth.
Every 78 seconds an adolescent attempts suicide.
Roughly every 90 minutes one succeeds.
Every 20 minutes an adolescent is killed in an accident.
Nearly half of all high school seniors have used an illegal drug at least once and almost 90% have used alcohol - some on a daily basis. [9]

On The Myth That Rape And Pornography Are Unrelated

Countries that have relaxed laws on pornography showed a marked increase in rape, according to a study made over the period 1964 to 1974. Australia was up 160 percent, the U.S. up 139 percent, New Zealand up 107 percent, and England up 94 percent. By contrast, a country like Singapore, which continued to limit pornography, showed only a 69 percent increase and Japan, which does not permit pornography, actually showed a 49 percent decrease in rape during the same period. [10]

Have we had enough of secular humanists promoting homosexual freedom between "consenting adults?" The consequences of homosexual promiscuity is an incurable AIDS epidemic which kills every one of its victims. It is threatening every single promiscuous individual (and even every monogamous partner of promiscuous partners)—and who knows what other virus vectors may develop which could put every human being on earth at risk—even Christians!

---

[8] Chalcedon Report, June 1986. Chalcedon, P O Box 158, Vallecito, CA 95251, [9] Quoted in *Christian Washington Letter*, February 1987., [10] Quoted in *Christian Washington Letter*, June 1986.

Discussing the implication of AIDS is a little like trying to prepare for a thermo-nuclear war. The best book available on AIDS is *The AIDS Coverup* by Gene Antonio, Ignatious Press, 1986. Don't read it standing up. Consider some of what is coming our way due to "gay rights" and "consenting adult" law.:

1. World health leaders are now talking about 100 million AIDS deaths worldwide.[11]
2. In four years New York City hospitals will be full up by serving *only* AIDS patients.[12]
3. Ten million Americans will likely die of AIDS by 2000 and it will cost $1.5 trillion to care for them.[13]

I won't go on to discuss possible infections by mosquitoes or blood or other nightmares. You'll be reading about it all soon enough in the front sections of your daily newspapers.

In "liberating" man from the biblical principles of morality, secularists are only condemning mankind to death. The earth will be controlled by one system of law or another: God's or man's. Which would you prefer? I am reminded of the choice that Moses set in front of Israel when He asked them which law base they wanted to follow, their own or God's:

See, I have set before you today life and prosperity, and death and adversity; in that I command you today to love the Lord your God, to walk in His ways and to keep His commandments and His statutes and His judgments, that you may live and multiply, and that the Lord your God may bless you in the land where you are entering to possess it. But if your heart turns away and you will not obey, but are drawn away and worship other gods and serve them, I declare to you today that you shall surely perish. You shall not prolong your days in the land where you are crossing the Jordan to enter and possess it. I call heaven and earth to witness against you today, that I have set before you life and death, the blessing and the curse. So choose life in order that you may live, you and your descendants (Deuteronomy 30:15-19).

---

[11] The Counsel Of Chalcedon, April-May, 1987, p. 34. [12] Ibid. p. 35. [13] Ibid., p. 35.

The following diagram should serve to further illustrate the point:

WHICH LAW BASE WILL COVER THE EARTH?

	THRONE OF GOD	*THRONE OF SELF-INTEREST*
Source:	GOD	SATAN
Administrator of Law:	THE CHURCH	SECULARIST LAW-SETTERS
Principles of Law:	THE KINGDOM OF GOD	WORLD SYSTEM WISDOM
	a. Christ's interests b. Revelation as supreme	a. Self interest b. Reason as supreme
Effect of the Law:	Order, freedom life, prosperity	Organized confusion, debt, perversion death
Ethics of the Law:	Honoring of, and service to the less able	Power and survival of the fittest

- Matthew 6:10
- Matthew 28:18-20
- Isaiah 42:4
- Psalm 89:14

Two law systems are battling for the rulership of the nations. The Marxists know this, the Shi'ite Moslems know this, and so do most people except, unfortunately, for naive Christians. All too often, we're the last on the block to know.

Man's laws are centered in human reason. They fulfill the scripture: "There is a way which seems right to a man, but its end is the way of death" (Proverbs 14:12).

Biblical Law Is Not Religious Tyranny

For too long Christians have not contradicted the secularist lie that pressing for biblical law will produce religious tyranny. Any time two or more persons attempt to interact with each other, some sort of rule system must be accepted for peaceful interaction and co-existence. Face it: any society will live by some sort of law. Biblical law is not only no more tyrannical than any law system, it is actually the only law system which preserves the dignity of the individual and the moral integrity of society. Was Egypt the tyrant over Israel, or was God's law? Was Assyria the tyrant over Israel, or was God's law? Was Babylon the tyrant over Israel or was God's law? Old Testament history records over and over again how the Israelites were in bondage every time they came under *man's law*, and were free only when they were obedient to God's law.

Biblical Law Means More than the Ten Commandments

The law, contrary to what many Christians think, goes far, far beyond the Ten Commandments. There are over two hundred legal issues in the scriptures, and nearly two-thirds of them have to do with how God's people were to order their culture politically or socially. I cannot overstate how important this point is.

Political commandments are the greatest number of commandments given in the whole Old Testament. Ordering a nation is not simple. Read Leviticus and Deuteronomy again. Follow how the prophets (Isaiah through Malachi) continually rebuked the Israelites for breaking those political laws, producing the gross injustice rampant in fallen Israelite society. The Psalms and Proverbs cannot be understood without understanding their continual references to the political law of God.

Jesus said that he did not come to do away with the Old Testament Law.[14] In addition to coming to die for our sins, He came to show us what God's law looks like when it is lived out by a man fully yielded to the Holy Spirit. God's law is perfect,[15] and the problems man has with living by the law are problems rooted in man's sinfulness, not in some imaginary flaw of the law itself. That law, which is fulfilled in Christ, is the foundation upon which Jesus operated. He did not try to do away with it; He made it

---

[92] Matthew 5:17-19 [93]. Psalm 19:7.

flesh and bone in His life.[16] Biblical laws are to be interpreted by the Holy Spirit, because the "Kingdom of God is in the Holy Spirit."[17]

The Church Should Exercise Judgment over the Nations

But what about the Bible's warning, "judge not?" Christians both hear and even espouse this context-bashing, misinterpretation of Jesus' words in Matthew 7:1 and 2 constantly. Get it straight: the Bible nowhere forbids biblical government, law enforcement, morality, or judgment either within the Christian Church or in the nations. Secular humanists, attempting to escape the coming wrath of God, and Christians attempting to escape their God-commanded responsibilities have unwittingly *banded together* in an unholy alliance to promote this fraud. Here's how the verse actually goes:

Judge not, that you be not judged. For with what judgment you judge, you will be judged; and with the same measure you use, it will be measured back to you (Matthew 7:1,2).

This passage is not forbidding judgment, it is warning that the one who affirms a system of judgment is *subject to that system* just as much as the person he wants to judge. In other words, the standard you use to judge others will be used to judge you. This is a warning. It isn't a warning not to render judgment. It's a warning not to render judgment by anything except God's law, or you will become a victim of your own faulty system! As a matter of fact, Jesus actually *tells* us to apply judgment in this oft-misquoted passage of Scripture:

First take the log out of your own eye, and then you will see clearly enough to take the speck out (exercise judgment) of your brother's (verse 5).

Do Christians look forward to the final judgment when God will erase the effects of sin? They say they do. Do Christians want their families and businesses protected from evildoers? They say they do. Do Christians want judges to render righteous judgment? They say they do. Then why don't they want their governments to

---

[16] John 1:14; Matthew 5:18,19   [17] Romans 14:17; 2 Corinthians 3:6

follow biblical law? Think about it, believers, if we can't face living under God's law *now*, what makes us eager to live under it in the world to come?

What About Grace And Compassion?

Conceding the point that Christians are to exercise judgment, what role does a gracious and forgiving spirit play in all of this? Are Christians supposed to act like "little Gods?" No, a thousand times, no! Christians are in no way intrinsically superior to non-Christians. What makes us different is how God views us and the person of the Holy Spirit within us. While Christians are exempt from the ultimate penalties for breaking the law, through Christ's redemption,[18] we are under obligation to live out its *principles* just like everybody else. Christians aren't superior, they are forgiven and empowered. They can still be weak, hypocrites and unloving, and it is this realization of our *own frailty* that must remove any haughtiness or *judgmental spirit* from us. *We don't pass judgment on anyone!* Only the Word does. We must apply God's Word, Jesus says, to all men — especially ourselves — but the *Word* exercises the judgment. There is a world of difference between holding up God's word as the standard of judgment and having a *judgmental spirit* ourselves. Christians have no such spiritual right for *God alone* is the judge of all men.

Do we apply the letter of the law or the spirit of God's law? What does the Word tell us? . . . "the letter kills, but the Spirit gives life" (2 Corinthians 3:6).

Judgment, Like Power, Is To Be Jurisdictional

How do the five governmental spheres of God's kingdom relate to judgment and law enforcement? Quite simply. The principle or spirit is this. The authority figures of each sphere teaches respect for and obedience to the biblical authority and standards of the other. Who enforces judgment? The legitimate authority the Bible designates over each of the five spheres. Who is that?

---

[18] Romans 10:4

Let's quickly see:

Self Government	• Man's spirit[19]
Family Government	• The Father[20]
Church Government	• Apostles, Prophets, Local Elders[21]
Commercial Government	• Employers[22]
Civil Government	• Power of Civil Courts[23]

Each one of these five leadership designates of course has a number of biblical injunctions upon it as to how it is to exercise authority in its sphere and the penalties for abuse of its judgmental authority. But the Bible doesn't empower the civil government to interfere in church government or church government to exercise authority in the family and so on. Biblical judgment is only properly applied within the jurisdictions the Bible grants. Commercial wages are not set by church elders, and Fathers do not directly enforce civil laws. The implications of this principle are immense.

Which Old Testament laws specifically apply today? Again the Scriptural patterns are clear - the revelation of the Old Testament is to be interpreted by the New.[24] While all Old Testament law is of principal value, all the laws dealing with *sacrifice* and *purification* are fulfilled in Christ[25] and all the laws dealing with food and the Sabbath and vengeance are specifically modified in the New Testament.[26] The breadth of the law in its entirety is a guideline and points to Christ. He fulfills both its penalties and releases its blessings for all believing mankind. This is the good news of the Gospel; the blessings of the law are mine in Christ Jesus.

Biblical Law Brings The Nations To Christ

The Church is commanded to bring the full gospel to the nations, explaining the consequent judgment which comes on those who reject any part of the gospel, and announcing reconciliation, redemption, and restoration through yielding to Christ.

The law is *for sinners* and is to be a *basis of judgment in our*

---

[19] Romans 1:9; Proverbs 16:32 [20] Genesis 18:19; Colossians 3:18-21 [21] Ephesians 2:20; 1 Thessalonians 5:12; Hebrews 13:7,17 [22] Colossians 3:22-25 [23] Romans 13:1-7 [24] Hebrews 1:1-2 [25] Hebrews 7-10 [26] Colossians 2:16-23; Matthew 5:38-40

civil society. As you read the following verses, no contrary interpretation does justice to the text. 1 Timothy 1:8-11 is the single most political statement in the New Testament as to the law-base God requires of all civil orders:

> *But we know that the Law is good, if one uses it lawfully,*
> *realizing the fact that law is not made for a righteous man,*
> *but for those who are lawless and rebellious, for the ungodly*
> *and sinners, for the unholy and profane, for those who kill*
> *their fathers or mothers, for murderers and immoral men*
> *and homosexuals and kidnappers and liars and perjurers,*
> *and whatever else is contrary to sound teaching, accor-*
> *ding to the glorious gospel of the blessed God, with which*
> *I have been entrusted* (1 Timothy 1:8-11).

Biblical law in the political realm not only brings civil order but *conviction* to the unrighteous as well.[27] It is Christ's law, principally applied to the culture, that will usher in the greatest revivals man has seen. The law is the Holy Spirit's crowbar to leverage convicted hearts.[28]

Judgment Has Been with Us From the Beginning

God intended for Adam to bring judgment against Satan and his angelic hosts by rejecting the temptation in the garden. Adam was free to choose that option. Man would have judged the angels. In fact, God still intends for Christians to render such judgment.

> *Do you not know that we shall judge angels? How much*
> *more, things that pertain to this life?* (1 Corinthians 6:3).

Christians are in training to become final judges through his word. We need to become experts in rendering judgment according to God's standards. After all, literally after all, we will judge the angels! Citizens of the kingdom, those who represent the Lord, you are called to exercise judgment in God's name.

To judge is to hold the plumbline of God's Word next to the activities of human beings, beginning with ourselves. Judgment must be made in every area of life, including civil judgment. Men are to judge themselves and their institutions by means of God's

---

[27] Galatians 3:24   [28] Romans 7:7

law, expressed in God's Word, the plumbline. Christians who fail to exercise their roles as political judges are living in disobedience to God and His Word.

God's Judgment in the Here and Now

Paul was upset. The Corinthian church was filled with dissension. They were even suing each other in the pagan Roman courts. They were seeking the moral judgment of pagan, godless judges between Christians, Christians who claimed to be under the law of the Creater God, the sovereign of the universe, yet they were stooping so low as to beg mercy at the seat of Roman law.

Paul was shocked:

"Does any one of you, when he has a case against his neighbor, dare to go to law before the unrighteous, and not before the saints? Or do you not know that the saints will judge the world? And if the world is judged by you, are you not competent to constitute the smallest law courts? Do you not know that we shall judge the angels? How much more, the matters of this life?"(1 Corinthians 6:1-3).

No scripture text, Old or New Testament, challenges Christians into political action and law setting more than this passage from the Apostle Paul. Paul is asking, in amazement, why the saints of Corinth don't know that they are supposed to be the source of legal interpretation for the church and others who would throw themselves at its mercy. As a result of Paul's admonition to set up Christian courts, the early Church did just that. The integrity of Christian judgment became so high that by the fourth and fifth centuries A.D., Christian courts became so superior to the Roman civil courts that even the unbelievers sought them out! As a matter of fact, the Roman emperors, by edict, began to ask the church elders who held these courts to put on the robes that the judges of the Roman courts has been wearing, in an attempt to regain the Roman citizens' faith in their own court system.

When Will We Obey And Judge?

What about today? Are the decisions of the civil government's courts "the matters of this life" that Paul exhorted you and me to judge? Are the criminal laws—and these laws are criminal—that abuse the victim and support the criminal "the matters of this life?" Is not our frequently absurd foreign policy "the matters of this life?" Is not the slaughter of the unborn and the corruption of our children "the matters of this life?" Are not the economic issues of the day "the matters of this life?" When will the church return to obedience and start judging "the matters of this life?" When will the church learn that you cannot have justice for man until you exercise Godly judgment on His behalf?

Christ has given His servants robes of righteousness, meaning righteous judgment as well as personal righteousness imputed by Christ's sacrifice on the cross. The Psalmist prophesied: "For judgment will again be righteous; and the upright in heart will follow it" (Psalm 94:15).

You and I have been redeemed. We are no longer forced to wear the shabby castoff garments of sinfulness, but can now choose the white robes of Christ's righteousness. Those righteous robes are not merely robes of salvation, robes that put us under His blood and let us into that heavenly City; but they are also judges' robes for those who have been elected to judge the matters of this life, the world and the angels!

To ban ourselves from our society and care only for the well being of those in our churches, is to condemn the world to death and deprive the unsaved of justice. God's holy principles are both a source of restraint to the unbelievers and a schoolmaster to lead them to Christ.[29] May the justice of His laws ring throughout the land!

Judges in Training

Don't despair. Don't be incredulous about your ability as a believer to judge the nations by effectively pressing for biblical standards as the basis for civil law. Gaining skills in rendering judgment takes years of practice. Like the training of a child it takes years of being under biblical law to learn to administer

---

[29] Galatians 3:24

biblical law. To grab the highest robes prematurely will only discredit the Church and God's law. We must begin in hope, knowing that the task is not insurmountable and is feasible in the power of Jesus Christ. Begin, as the early Church did, to become accomplished local judges—citizens rendering judgment in the voting booth and precinct and school boards—before we attempt to become Supreme Court justices! We need to get into training now, in confidence that we will rule later on.[30] We need to apprentice locally before we enter the international political Olympics.

Judging Ourselves As We Judge The Nations

God will bring final judgment when Christ physically returns to earth. Now His Church is called to bring *progressive judgment* to the nations as it cleanses them. What a responsiblity and what a blessing!

So why hasn't the Church wanted to shoulder its responsibilies to judge? I believe the answer is simple: we have feared being judged *ourselves* by God,[31] or even by the world's system. Exercising judgment forces you to clean up your own act as Jesus told us in Matthew 7:1-3. A "bride that has made herself ready"[32] is a bride that has begun the purifying process of judging the nations and is therefore being purified by God's judgments as well as the purifying attacks from the world system. We have nothing to fear from either God's judgment or the faulty judgment of the world. Both of them are a gift to us to bring us to be a matured companion fit to rule at Christ's side. But we must "pull the trigger" of judgment in order to release the cleansing flow.

Rejoice! We have been judged clean by Christ's blood. It is time to take our rightful place as lights of justice and righteousness in the midst of the nations. Can we put Christ's morality on the nations? Absolutely! For His morality is filled with truth and justice and mercy is its heart:

A bruised reed He will not break
And a dimly burning wick He will not extinguish

---

[30] Revelation 2:26-27   [31] 1 Peter 4:17   [32] Revelation 19:7

He will not be disheartened or crushed,
Until He has established justice in the earth;
And the coastlands will wait expectantly for His law
(Isaiah 42: 3-4).

From the rising of the sun, even to its setting, My name will be great among the nations

(Malachi 1:11)

CHAPTER SIX

Politics Doesn't Have to be a Dirty Business

The leaders of the world system fear Christians becoming political for many reasons, some of some of which we have already discussed. But why is *politics* so sacred to them? Why do they fear our involvement there above everything else? Because the political arena is their instrument of power, their "headquarters." It enables them to perpetuate the organized abuse of the many by the few. It is their power base. They have bought into their own propaganda that civil government is the most important form of all governments. Politics is their religion.

They attack the Church's political involvement on *theological grounds* because they know that the Church acts out of theological conviction. Our enemy dons the appearance of one concerned for the Church's moral purity and warns us that "politics is a dirty business" that "will corrupt the Church." "Stick to winning souls," he says. His reasoning is simple: he wants the Church far, far away from the immoral concentration camps into which he is herding the nations!

Christian Politics Is Loving And Serving People

The central truth of the gospel is involvement with people. Relating to and caring for people is what living out our Christian commitment in love is all about.[1] To deny Christians the

---

[1] 1 John 4:7, 20, 21; James 1:27

right to involvement, sacrifice, and love for others through political service is to deny the heart of our faith. Jesus commissioned us to love and serve others this way:

> *This is My commandment, that you love one another, just as I have loved you. Greater love has no one than this, that one lay down his life for his friends. You are My friends, if you do what I command you ... This I command you, that you love one another* (John 15:12-17).

If you don't get involved on behalf of others—in all areas of the ordering of human life, including politics—you're simply not obeying the Lord's commandment. It's that simple.

"He that would be greatest among you must be the servant of all" (Matthew 23:11). Dominion is through service, not tyranny, as Christ kept reminding his disciples.[2] If you want to lead, you must serve. You lead by serving. If you don't want to lead, then you are saying that you don't want to serve. Leadership is inescapable for those who serve faithfully.

Death To Personal Ambition

The politics of Christ is death to personal ambition, and the courage to do what is right, even when it is unpopular. The citizen of God's kingdom must live and preach a gospel that is centered in serving God and others. Today, much of politics is the game of getting what will further serve oneself. Christians must bring a different spirit into the marketplace of laws and power. The Christian voice must rise above the level of denominational doctrinal disputes and, instead, unite around the indisputables of serving the world around us.

The nations can be rescued only by people who will give their lives to free others from the prison of self-centeredness. Christians must cease from being self-serving and instead find their lives through serving others.

Psalm 67 deals clearly with the servant motivation of the citizen of the kingdom as he operates in the political realm:

---

[2] Matthew 20:27; 23:11; 25:21-30; 34-46

A DIRTY BUSINESS

"God be gracious to us and bless us, that Thy way may be known on the earth, Thy salvation among the nations" (Psalm 67:1, 2).

God gives us this kind of grace, not to be spent on ourselves, but instead to be given to the Church, so that we will be empowered to make God's ways known on the earth. The Psalmist declares that the nations (political societies of the earth) need the salvation of God as much as do unredeemed individuals. The nations are waiting for the servants of the kingdom to break forth from their isolated church ghettos and channel the grace and life of God into the public marketplace.

Jesus came to serve, not to use His power and His office for personal gain. Let the Church imitate this politically, girding ourselves with the towel of Christ's humility as we cleanse the nations with God's liberating Word.

The World System Doesn't Want Our Political Service

The nations are imprisoned primarily because Christians have done one of two foolish things: (1) they have attempted to withdraw from the issues of human life altogether so they could get "spiritual;" or (2) when they *have* exercised their political duties, they have left their Christian convictions out of their politics. As a result, they have made no better impact on government than any other Democrat, Republican, Libertarian, or other political party animal. They have frequently voted by party affiliation and not by biblical principle.

"Religious" systems seem to enjoy retreat and isolation. Pharisees love to separate themselves from the "normal" everyday world of people. Jesus was continuously persecuted by the church leaders of his day for being "worldly" as he hung around with sinners of the commonest sort. They said he was too involved with people to be truly holy. Not much has changed; the religious system resents people-lovers.

Here come the secularists, the ACLU-ers, the "Christian" Pharisees, the "religionists", all spouting their own form of Satan's lie that Christians just can't get involved in what is intrinsically "dirty." Listen to their lying litany:

"Politics by its very nature is dirty: It just can't be cleaned up. Not before the second coming of Christ, anyway. Then He'll run the whole show, top to bottom. Civil government will be mostly bureaucracy then, sort of like an army. Christians will just follow orders.

Politics is corrupting. It takes Christians into realms of power and compromise that are totally at odds with their call to be separate and holy. It deals with worldly issues and earth-type problems. Leave it alone and keep your eyes on heaven."

No matter what the chant, the terms are always the same: stay out of our game. Leave the power to us. Keep out of the way!

Politics Doesn't Have to Be Dirty

And a voice came to him, "Rise, Peter; kill and eat." But Peter said, "Not so, Lord! For I have never eaten anything common or unclean." And a voice spoke to him again the second time, "What God has cleansed you must not call common" (Acts 10:12-14).

What religious man calls "unclean" is not the issue; what matters is how God views the matter. Since civil government (politics) is ordained by Him, we must "rise and eat" even if the commonness of the political order offends our Christian sensibilities.

Politics is the ordering of civil institutions. To the citizen of the kingdom of God, political involvement is as much required of him as his involvement in family life or the life of the Church. This is a revolutionary statement and one that, if thought through, could well change the earth. It is built upon the truth that God requires His servants to rule in life in all five of His orders of government: self-government, family government, Church government, commercial government and civil government—politics.

The first and most general reason Christians need to be involved in politics is that politics is part of God's creation. If the earth belongs to Him, then so does the realm of politics. The government of the earth is on his shoulders, not Satan's.[3] Think about it: How long should Christians let Satan shoulder Christ's governing of the nations?

Family Rule Isn't Always A Dirty Business?

To see just how nonsensical such arguments are, substitute the word "family" for "politics." Are we prepared to argue that family life is a dirty business? Husbands cheat on wives, wives cheat on husbands, kids run wild, and families are in debt up to their ears (just like the federal government!). Couples promise to be faithful to each other, but they have their fingers crossed. Almost half of their marriages end in divorce, and if the divorce laws get much looser, more of them will.

Is this an accurate view of the family? Is the family by nature unclean? Is your family by nature unclean? Can't family life be cleaned up by the grace of God? Aren't families constantly being restored to wholeness before God through His grace, and then by their faithful obedience to God? Of course they are!

Families are a form of God's government. Parents discipline children. Husbands are supposed to exercise godly judgment. God's ultimate authority is displayed to us in the family. Church leaders are first supposed to demonstrate their *ability to rule their families* in good order before they are chosen to lead their congregations.[4]

If family government can be brought under the dominion of Christ, why not civil government? Why is politics innately dirty? Politics is the legal process by which people bring civil government under dominion, either to God or Satan. In God's sight, civil government is no less *His* than family government.

Church Rule Isn't Always Dirty?

We can make churches just as dirty as politics. Why don't we accept the following negative generalizations? "Churches are filled with hypocrites. Ministers are all on ego trips. A handful of people

[3] Isaiah 9:6-7. [4] 1 Timothy 3:1-5

lord it over the members. It's all a big power play, but it's hidden in a lot of religious sounding talk. It's all fake. It's a dirty business. It's worse than politics because it's all phony. At least politics is honestly dirty."

We've all heard some variation of these arguments. Why don't we believe them? Because none of these charges ever apply? No, sometimes they do. Sometimes. But they don't apply most of the time in most churches.

The Church, like the family, is a government. There are rules to follow, and a chain of command. There are events called excommunications where law-breakers and rebels are removed from the camp of the faithful. There are also events called baptisms, where people are brought openly into the camp of the faithful. There are elections in many churches. In short, the Church looks like a government because it is a government—a special kind of government.

Now, is all church government dirty? Of course not! Then why do we say that all political government is dirty just because some of it is dirty? Why can't civil government be cleaned up through political action—Christian political action?

Every legitimate government has rules for attaining greater lawful authority and justice. Every government has a jurisdiction (a rule of law). There is a process through which men attain power. The goal is to bring this process of attaining rule under the requirements God has for each form of government. In the Church, for example, the personal requirements for lawful candidates for church offices are explained in 1 Timothy 3. For civil government, these personal requirements are explained in Exodus 18. In both cases, the requirements are moral. There are requirements. Justice and righteousness require them from every government man touches.

Then why do Christians refuse to get involved in restructuring the process of civil politics? The answer: deception, ignorance, and irresponsibility.

But it can change, it should change, and it will change—with a Church committed to fulfilling God's commandments in every aspect of life.

A DIRTY BUSINESS

Cleaning up the Mess

The reason politics seems so much dirtier than family or church is that we haven't tried cleaning it up yet. Why are the family and the church less dirty than politics? Because long ago Christians got involved in family life and church life. Because Christians determined that these two areas of government belonged to God, and that they were to be operated in terms of God's revealed principles, found in the Bible. And they were right.

Politics isn't innately dirty, any more so than family or church government. And we should clean it up just the same way we clean up dirty, faltering families and dirty, faltering churches: by a faithful proclamation and institution of the whole gospel, including the announcement of the unchanging standards of God.

We should declare the crown rights of King Jesus in every area of life—just like the humanists do for the supposed crown rights of "King Man."

Politics and Christian Citizenship

So then you are no longer strangers and aliens, but you are fellow citizens with the saints, and are of God's household (Ephesians 2:19).

The Apostle Paul tells us how Christians are to approach their identity as those who dwell in God's household. They are to see themselves as *citizens* of the kingdom of God. That citizenship entails privileges, obligations and responsibilities. "Citizen" is a political word, not a church word, but Paul used it to describe the believer's status in the kingdom of God.

To be a well-balanced citizen in the kingdom, we must function biblically in each one of the spheres as scripture commands us. That God is vitally involved with political issues is easily demonstrated from the Bible:

1. God ordained civil governments[5]
2. God established the rulers over nations[6]
3. Therefore, he commands our obedience to civil rulers[7]

---

[5] Romans 13:1; Daniel 2:21   [6] Psalm 47:7; 75:7; Daniel 2:21   [7] Romans 13:1-3

4. Jesus legitimized civil government by urging us to pay taxes to them[8]

5. God has carefully set out the limitations on civil government He requires:

    a. God commands the rulers of the nations to rule on God's terms[9]

    b. Civil law must be founded upon God's law[10]

    c. Civil officials must be elected representatives by the people[11]

The Covenant Of Peace

These scriptures teach that the basis of civil authority is *covenantal* in nature. This means that citizens of the kingdom of God are both to be responsible to the civil authority, and to judge the performance of the civil authority as the Church holds the nations of the earth accountable to the standards of God's Word. The Church is not to *rule* civil government (theocracy) but it is to demand that civil government obey Christ's commandments.[12]

This also leads the citizen of the kingdom of God to the inescapable conclusion that, since politics is God-ordained, it is a sin for a Christian to refuse involvement in it. I am not saying all Christians should run for or hold a political office. I am saying that all Christians should vote, speak out on issues, promoting what is righteous (light) and working against what is ungodly (judgment); and challenge all leaders and institutions of society to obey biblical principles as they are entrusted with the responsibility of civil government.

These Christian duties will require much prayer and study of the issues for us to serve men wisely. But sacrifice is the stuff of which real love is made. Christian caring will bring the same cleansing to civil government as it brings to the other four governments. And love is manifested by the commitment to work hard and long to enhance what one loves. Let's go to work and start washing the dirt out of the system. Dirty politics requires the

---

[8] Matthew 22:15-22 [9] Psalm 2:10-11; Luke 18:2,6; 3:19-20; Acts 5:29 [10] Psalm 2:10-12; Isaiah 33:22; Deuteronomy 4:2-9; 1 Timothy 1:8-10 [11] Deuteronomy 1:13,15,17 [12] Matthew 28:18-19

same cleansing agent as the dirty church — the application of God's Word:

> Husbands, love your wives, just as Christ also loved the church and gave Himself up for her;
>
> that He might sanctify her, having cleansed her by the washing of water with the word (Ephesians 5:25-26).

My people are destroyed for lack of knowledge. Because you have rejected knowledge, I will also reject you from being My priest. Since you have forgotten the law of your God, I also will forget your children

(Hosea 4:6)

CHAPTER SEVEN

Attacking The Lies That Are Stealing Our Children's Future

G od always has drawn leaders to Himself to equip them for use in delivering His people. These leaders must be "de-programmed" from the surrounding pagan propaganda for them to have the necessary vision to lead others into freedom. Abraham was called away from his home in Ur; Moses was called away from Pharaoh's household; Daniel was called from among the king's court; David from the fields of his people to those of the Philistines, from the towns to the caves; John the Baptist from the desert to the river Jordan; Jesus from the wilderness; and Paul from the ranks of the Pharisees. It is almost impossible to see clearly in the midst of the "system." The world's system is designed to keep us blind.

You don't think you can be a Christian and be brainwashed? Look at what we're up against. Over six billion dollars was spent last year (1986) by the television industry to keep us viewing life as the entertainment moguls see it. The world has evangelized the Church far more than the Church has evangelized the world. The net result is Christians with saved souls but clouded minds filled with the secularized opinions of the world. The world has told us to withdraw from ruling on the earth, cut a "deal" with them, stay clean from impacting the culture and don't try to scale the wall of church-state separation. We bought their program with scarcely a whimper. Having effectively deceived us, the world is now in deadly pursuit of our children and grandchildren's minds, knowing that whoever controls the minds of the children, controls the future.

Rescuing Our Children

We must rescue our children from the cultural lies that attack them in our public schools and the media. We must find a way for Christian tax dollars to be diverted from self-destructiveness. We must stop supporting a public school system that trains children to abandon and even attack our Christian values, using our money to do it. It is suicide for Christians to subsidize secular humanism's public school system through our taxes. Christian schools and home schools, as essential as they are, avoid this issue: they don't deal with this problem of self-administered poison through public school taxation.

Preliminary to effectively standing up for our rights, Christians must first equip themselves with God's word, learning to see the ultimate issues that make up a Christian view of life and culture. We must stop feeding on the world's rations and swallowing its poison.

As Christians who see the need to make a difference in our world we must understand and confront the six major deceptions preached in our secular culture against us and our children. Conquering these six lies in the power and authority of Christ will liberate our society from the strangle hold of secular humanism.

Lie Number One: There Are No Absolutes

Fallen man is a moral coward. He hides from God's absolutes and judgment either by denying their existence, or by rebelling from them, establishing *his own standards*. Modern man is the greatest coward of all: he systematically destroys any values in his culture which challenge him with either personal restraint or personal guilt.

Anyone in such a culture who dares to promote biblical values is held up to ridicule and viewed as an idiot. They are seen as "bigots" and "fascists"—the "far Christian Right." Christians are *automatically* wrong because they are speaking in absolute terms.

This mentality is a cruel lie, abandoning reason and reality for the deceitful comfort of irrational fantasy. The lack of absolute cultural standards has turned our society into a gutless shell.

Does anyone have guts any more? Is anyone willing to fight to protect society from reprobates whose only abilities are to kill, maim and destroy? Who is ready to challenge these reprobates even to the point of some of them curtailing their civil rights in the interest of justice and the sheer survival of our society? Is our society really this spineless, or are we just living out some kind of Mad Hatter's Tea Party?

The point is this: when you lose absolutes, you lose the courage to act with absolute and final action. The sad result is that criminality multiplies and our society becomes polarized into the predators and the prey. We can't let that go on. We must identify, locate, and eradicate the following five deadly aspects of culture-permeating relativism:

A. *The loss of absolutes produces "the cult of self."* When the moral absolutes of the universe are trashed, some new false gods will inevitably try to take their places. Man must have standards even if they are self-created ones. The standard of ultimate value in our increasingly decadent culture is this: personal self-expression is the highest goal of life.

The cult of self argues that since man is not good or bad, his ultimate goal becomes maximizing his personal goals and pleasures and minimizing whatever tries to restrain him. If it feels good, do it; if you want it, take it; if you can't afford it, charge it; if it makes you feel guilty, get rid of it. Personal freedom is god and all others are objects to be sacrificed on the altar of self-exploration and self-satisfaction.

Men rape to satisfy their "needs," women serving as convenient consumer goods. Judges and lawmakers are squeezed between compassion for the victim and a culturally dictated "responsibility" to "help" the rapist "to learn a more socially acceptable form of self-expression." That's insane! The victim needs help. The rapist needs punishment.

Thirty thousand children disappear annually, many of them drawn into the world of kiddie porn. Annual child porn sales last year? Over $500 million. But we're exhorted not to be so judgmental. The sex offender has a need to express himself too, we're told.

The game is simple: prey on the weak, maximize your options, conceal your motives, and attack the lunatic fringe (Christians) who want to bring another rule book into the game. In this survival of the fittest world, *love* is defined as *toleration* and *hate* as being judgmental *with absolutes*. How perfectly this modern situation fulfills the scripture:

> *Woe to those who call evil good, and good evil; Who substitute darkness for light and light for darkness; who substitute bitter for sweet, and sweet for bitter* (Isaiah 5:20).

Until this cult of self is exposed and rejected, it won't ultimately matter who becomes our next president or governor or judge. The corrupt value system itself is far more powerful in evil than its leaders could be in good. Ideas are bigger than men or institutions.

B. The loss of absolutes destroys the ultimate value of human life. When we discard the truth that man is created in the image of God, with intrinsic and unique value, then hell opens up its jaws to gaping proportions. Blacks become "niggers," Jews become "gene polluters," unborn babies become "fetal tissue," old people become "sufferers," the abnormal become "less than quality of life humans," and all non-Marxists become "enemies of the state." Cut the anchor to man's created value and you condemn the underdogs of society to the cruel judgments of the powerful, who have the power to decide who will live, die, or be oppressed.

If people are simply the organized "goop" of the evolutionary process, why not exercise *the power of the fittest?* If I can gain power over you, doesn't that give me the *right* of power? In a society where evolution is taught as reality, power over others becomes the supreme law of the entire social structure. Evolution sets power as god, telling us that survival of the powerful is the inexorable goal of existence.

Should Christians demand a creation view of man—one that esteems each man's dignity—be taught to the youth of the culture? It's the only option if we want freedom from the view of life that increasingly rationalizes killing people because they are inferior, inconvenient, or powerless.

C. *The loss of absolutes gives us laws that reject justice and instead produce criminals.* Is there "justice for all" in America? Or does crime really pay? Why have our crime rates gone through the ceiling in the last 25 years? It's easy to understand. When man's laws are set by man, in direct *opposition* to God's absolute laws, the society must then promote the rebellion and disdain for others which produced the criminals in the first place. Legal constitutions or criminal systems produce what they are. If the laws of a whole society reject God's ultimate laws, and become *codified criminality* in the universe, all that society can produce is more criminals. The state that breaks God's laws will produce citizens who break their state's laws. Everything produces fruit "after its own kind."[1]

Our nation's Constitution was established upon the principles of English common law, itself based on biblical law. But in the late 19th century, the teachings of "scientific evolutionary thought" became a weapon of secularists in their rebellion against God's absolutes. They convinced our nation's judges that our Constitution was not a "fixed" document. They argued that our Constitution's principles should be interpreted by today's evolving standards rather than by the timeless standards of God's word. The result is that the interpretation of the United States Constitution today is a relative rubber band rather than a dependable yardstick. Judges make it mean what they think the prevailing culture wants it to mean. And who determines what the "prevailing culture" is? The media. In a culture where constitutional law is relative, public policy becomes the law of the land, and the media —the Supreme Court.

---

[1] Genesis 1:11, 12, 21, 24

Are you as a Christian, afraid to impose God's laws on other men? Take a good look at the closing walls of evolutionary law that are moving to crush us, with less than a whimper from most of us deluded victims. Is this criminal and relativistic law base what you want to give to your children for their social heritage? Not if you really love your kids.

D. The loss of absolutes produces unstable and dangerous foreign policies. Dangerous people or nations are the ones whose behavior under stress is unpredictable. When a nation's moral fiber is removed because it no longer acts upon absolute standards, it becomes very dangerous. The United States is now in this unpredictable position, and its zig-zag foreign policy poses a major threat to world stability. Our double-mindedness has made us an unreliable world partner.

We are like an unstable landowner who meets his mortal enemy at the borders of his property. He says to his enemy, "If you cross over my property line, I will shoot you." And then he watches his enemy cross over the line. The farmer then says, "OK, if you come one hundred yards closer, it's all over." The enemy advances. "This time I really mean it," says the farmer. "Come within the yard and I'll shoot." The enemy advances. He is now breaking down the farmer's front door, having shot his livestock and set fire to his crops! The farmer is finished. His enemy advanced when no absolute response was enforced. Examples? Eastern Europe, Vietnam/Cambodia, Korea, Cuba, many African nations, Nicaragua. Our enemies advance, we draw more meaningless lines.

Foreign policy reflects the internal values and resolve of a nation. You export what you are. What does the United States foreign policy reflect? Confusion, duplicity and division. Why? Because we are a nation with a divided heart, which is God's judgment on us. When a nation loses its absolutes, it becomes a prisoner to any other nation that still has them. We are held hostage around the world because the Marxists and the Moslem terrorists have absolutes and are willing to die for them.

E. The loss of absolutes takes with it the ability to learn from history. Understanding God's absolute laws is the key to

interpreting history. In history we can see the blessings of obedience to reality or the consequences of ignoring it. The nation
that loses the ability to see absolutes loses the meaning of where
it has been and consequently the foundations upon which it can
build for its future. The judgment of God upon a people that has
lost touch with his natural and universal laws is a punitive sentence
served behind bars of weakness, isolation, and helplessness.

History should be a tool to growth. To the godless it becomes
a meaningless nothing. This cruel deception of our historical
rootlessness leads us further into the abyss of men separated from
the values of their heritage and traditions. They are lost, unable
to see where they are going because they cannot see where they
have been.

**Lie Number Two: *Today* Is Everything—The Past and Its Peo-
ple Are Nothing.**

> *Do not move the ancient boundary which your fathers have
> set* (Proverbs 22:28).
> *Remember the law of Moses My servant, even the statutes
> and ordinances which I commanded him in Horeb for all
> Israel. Behold, I am going to send you Elijah the prophet
> before the coming of the great and terrible day of the Lord.
> And he will restore the hearts of the fathers to their children,
> and the hearts of the children to their fathers, lest I come
> and smite the land with a curse* (Malachi 4:4-6).

All societies or nations must implant a sense of destiny in their
children in order to survive. Living only for oneself guarantees
eventual poverty and imprisonment for one's descendants. A
godless society is a selfish society; the fathers do not invest in
the future for their children. They consume their children's
resources and spend them upon themselves. They produce the
"curse" that Malachi describes above. This curse is threatening
the United States and the entire Western world right now. We are
becoming nations under a curse because vast numbers of our
citizens live only for themselves and say, "Charge it! Leave the
bill for our children."

Consume, consume, chomp, chomp. Let's all go to heaven and

leave the bills and debris to the anti-Christ. Fine. But what if three generations of our posterity precede him? This isn't occupying until Christ comes or loving our children and our children's children. It's raw selfishness and sin.

We Must Return To Generational Thinking

Generational thinking is the key to wealth because the sustained faithfulness and sacrifice of the parents passes on accumulated wisdom and resources to their children. Divorce produces poverty, as does consumption beyond savings. Parents who don't think generationally consume rather than create wealth. Their children pay the price. Men who father illegitimate children condemn them to poverty and the humiliation of being cared for by the state. An easy way to measure the health of a nation is to count the rate and direction if its divorces, abortions, and illegitimacies. It will tell you if the nation loves its children and is planning to pass on to them more than was given to the present generation.

Guess how we stack up? Our nation is generationally bankrupt. How can we pass freedom and wealth on to our children if we are convinced that Jesus is going to rescue us from an evil world any second and that we need not plan for our children's future? We are to "love His appearing," but we are to do so in a way that "occupies till He comes" and fulfills these commandments as well:

> *He that provides not for his own is worse than an unbeliever and has denied the faith* (1 Timothy 5:8).
> *Children ought not to lay up for the parents, but parents for the children* (2 Corinthians 12:14).

I am asking you, in Jesus' Name, to change the future: live in such a way so as to *give your children* more true freedom than your parents gave you, and to give them the accumulation of your increased resources. Following your example they will believe in and love their own children's futures as well. You will have shown them how.

Lie Number Three: The State Is the Source of Man's Rights.

Freedom is living in obedience to God's laws. Disobedience brings confusion, unreality, poverty and imprisonment. While man can take certain freedoms from his fellow man, he cannot make other men free. Freedom is something each man and woman must secure, by God's help, for himself. Each generation must decide for itself the price it is willing to pay to live in obedience to God, unrestrained by sin or the tyrannical government of other men.

The founders of our nation, firmly committed to absolute and divinely guaranteed freedoms, understood these truths and built them into our founding documents. Our Declaration of Independence states the reality and source of all true freedom:

We hold these truths to be self-evident; that all men are endowed by their creator with certain inalienable rights, among which are life, liberty and the pursuit of happiness.

The political battle of our age centers on this issue; whom must the state obey? If it is really God (the final power and authority of men and law on earth), as the secular-humanist religions of socialism maintain, then those *men* who politically rule the state are God. The battle for the nations hinges on this question: Does man look to other men to determine his ultimate rights, or to his maker? This nation once possessed the right answer. Now, in its increasing rejection of God's laws, it is moving toward the same imprisonments of all other godless societies that worship the power of man's laws.

We are told that freedom is given or taken away by the power of the state. That the state is given the responsibility to rule in civil issues on God's behalf is not in question. Paul tells us this in Romans 13:1-2:

Let every person be in subjection to the governing authorities. For there is no authority, except from God, and those which exist are established by God. Therefore he who resists authority has opposed the ordinance of God; and they who have opposed will receive condemnation upon themselves (Romans 13:1-2).

But the state cannot control for its citizens the rights that God alone dispenses. Marxism tells us that the state is God walking on the earth, the state is where the possibility for true freedom is embodied. The state is the "will of the people" as determined by the philosopher-bureaucrat. The state tells the Church what it will and will not teach or where it will or will not meet. What is best for society, it says, is for religion to be removed from public life. The state says it has the right to so determine. It knows what is best for the people because it is the voice of the people.

We all must learn one thing: freedom is a gift given by God to those who choose to be free by clinging to the cross, even at the threat of death. Jesus died to secure our freedom. In a lesser way, countless thousands have followed Him by giving up their lives to secure freedom for us in both war and peace. The state rules by our permission and its only *right* is to obey the founding documents to which it looks for a statement of its authority.

Lie Number Four: Governments Can Create Wealth by Printing Money.

Your silver has become dross
Your drink diluted with water
Your rulers are rebels (Isaiah 1:22,23).

When man plays God, the first thing he does is to organize his disobedience into public laws. The second thing he does is to create new wealth without work by making more diluted currency. Since God can create wealth out of nothing (Jesus and the multiplied loaves and fishes, for example), rebellious man tries to counterfeit the same in imitation.

Wealth is created by two things: obedience to God's laws and sustained work. A pay increase that is not built upon more productive labor or higher real profits is an economic sin. This unjustified "raise" will be paid for by everybody else simply to reinforce the illusion of wealth. Our nation gives itself many illusory "raises" by increasing the money supply with no increased productivity or value to support it. This watering down of our currency not only destroys the fixed incomes of the aged, it also

100

prices the young out of the same American dreams their parents were able to earn.

At the root of this problem is the loss of the good old-fashioned work ethic. Why work hard if you can get a raise on negotiated contracts divorced from increased productivity? Instead of believing we have a right to give an honest day for an honest pay, Americans have been told that they have a "right" to an ever-increasingly comfortable life-style. Who says so? Not God. His revealed values contradict this myth of modern economic values. He says we are to work on our jobs "as unto Him" and that a blessed life-style comes from obedience to his Word.[2] In today's heading-over-the-cliff world, we equate increased productivity with more paper money and don't believe we have to work harder, we just have to get paid more for less. This debt-producing policy is deadly and leaves a devastating inheritance for our children.

It's pure fantasy to think you can spend yourself rich and create wealth by operating a printing press more often. When the bill eventually comes due, our children of that generation will have every right to disown us.

Lie Number Five: All Men Should Be Equal Partners in Privilege and Wealth.

All men are created by God equal in their responsibility to obey Him, but they are not created equal in talents, resources, or environment. But when man sets himself up to be God, he tries to make equal what God made unequal or different. The myth that all men should have equal incomes or shares of land is unbiblical. It produces injustice, theft, mediocrity, and economic stagnation. All men should have *access* to provide for themselves according to their abilities and no more. Christian duty in the realm of economic justice is to enable men to increase their skills and productivity and to care for those who cannot care for themselves. It is insanity to join with the Marxists in producing a classless society of gray mediocrity and organized theft and inefficiency.

The modern secular humanist, in his misplaced zeal to be God,

---
[2] Deuteronomy 20:1-12

extends a kind of compassion that actually enslaves his brother. Instead of teaching him to fish, he gives him fish—perpetuating his dependency and inflating the paternalistic ego of the giver. If you truly love someone, you will lead him into an understanding of how God's laws work. You will help him become dependent upon his resources in God, not you. The state, since it can only imitate God, cannot do this. It must create dependence upon it, not upon God. It creates wards of the state in the name of compassion.

Isn't exploitation ungodly? Yes, and the Bible soundly condemns it. But exploitation can only be overcome when man stops exploiting by becoming a servant. Christianity promotes the only truly servant ethic on the earth. What keeps people and nations poor is not just exploitation by others. What keeps them poor is disobedience to God's laws. American so-called "capitalist exploitation" has far less to do with world poverty than the overwhelming truth that bondage is produced by covetousness, laziness, immorality, family disintegration, lack of savings, and slack use of resources and labor.

Christian liberators must extend true compassion. Out of the fruit of their own obedience and increase, they must help other men to stand on their own feet rather than depending on a handout to perpetuate a lifetime of poverty.

May God help us to be compassionate! May He deliver us from a philosophy of life that kills our brothers by making them unnaturally and permanently dependent on other men under the guise of equality.

Lie Number Six: Science Can Free Man from the Limits of Sexual Restraint.

The laws of God's nature enforce His laws of morality even if law makers in society won't. Ultimately, you don't break God's laws, they break you. One of modern secular man's greatest hopes was to use science to rescue him from monogamous sex. He thought he had it made and is still whistling in the dark as deadly sexually transmitted disease hunts him down.

Children are told by our secular antagonists that the pill gives them freedom. What it really gives is incredible peer pressure and often deadly medical side effects. Abortion? Go for it. Only now women's delayed physical and emotional injuries from abortion are rapidly appearing. Emancipated and sexually free from uptight Christian morals? Today we are overwhelmed by sexually transmitted diseases, including 22 million cases of incurable herpes. Homosexuality is true freedom? Today it is freedom to be a victim of the greatest medical holocaust since the "Black Death" of the Middle Ages, its practitioners and their sometimes innocent partners guaranteed death from AIDS. And our public-funded health care system is almost guaranteed bankruptcy in trying to care for AIDS patients.

Love In Action

If you truly love your children or grandchildren, don't just read these sentences and agree with me—do something! Go out and *mobilize* to rescue the children of the next generations from these deadly lies! If you don't know who to work with, write us.*

---

* See Appendix A for additional information including how to locate Christian activist groups.

A wise man scales the city of the mighty, and brings down the stronghold in which they trust

(Proverbs 21:22)

CHAPTER EIGHT

Storming the Gates Of Our Cities

C hristians have lost control of the issues and moral foundations by which the cities of this land should be ruled. Instead of sitting in the seats of power and establishing the agendas for men's social order, we have needlessly become the ruled rather than the rulers.[1] We have, unfortunately, earned our right to irrelevancy. We have ceased to operate as salt and light within our nation's cities and instead have withdrawn into our Christian ghettos, fulfilling the Master's words:

> *But if the salt has become tasteless...it is good for nothing anymore, except to be thrown out and trampled under foot by men* (Matthew 5:13).

The Church cannot disciple and lead the nations if it is constantly in retreat! Rulers don't run, and runners don't rule. We have been so preoccupied with getting ready to leave the planet, that were we to actually meet the Lord in the air now, I wouldn't be surprised if the world hardly noticed we were gone!

Jesus' Church should be victorious and on the offensive. Nobody in retreat was ever victorious. Only armies that march forward find victory. Christian liberators are men and women who believe that Jesus was right when He said, "I will build My Church; and the gates of Hell shall not prevail against it" (Matthew 16:18).

---

[1] Deuteronomy 28:44

Guardians of the City

Our cities are administrated by those who have convinced a majority of the voting people that they should be elected. The ongoing record of corruption, violence, and the plight of the genuinely needy is a clear statement that these elected officials are not guarding the gates of our cities very well.

How many Christians did you see running for office on your last election ballot? How many men of "elder" quality did you see asking for your vote of confidence on their ability to rule over those gates and provide both safety and justice for you? They're almost non-existent because they don't know they're supposed to be there. Most Christians have lost sight of the kingdom and failed to take the gospel to the institution of civil government. We have not obeyed the "Great Commission"[2] to teach the nations to obey His laws.

God's Leaders Protect the Cities

Leaders in Old Testament Israel understood their political responsibility "to sit in the gates of the city," overseeing the quality of life within. This honor was the ultimate civil place of esteem. The virtuous woman of Proverbs 31 held as her greatest treasure the fact that her husband "sat in the gates of the city," a sign of the Lord's favor upon them both.[3]

The elders judged as the duly constituted legal rulers. God held those elders responsible both for the continued well-being of the citizens and also for protecting the citizens from evil without the gates. If the thief or the unscrupulous businessman destroyed or cheated the inhabitants of the city, the inhabitants had the right to challenge the elders as to why such men were let into the city in the first place. The elders were God's first line of defense for the safety and welfare of the people.[4]

Do you feel your elected officials are concerned primarily with your safety and welfare? Hardly. We are not exerting our moral leadership in our nation's cities, bringing the issues of justice and righteousness into the streets according to the biblical mandate.

[2] Matthew 28:18-20 [3] Proverbs 31:23 [4] Deuteronomy 19:11-12; Isaiah 20:4; Proverbs 8:1-3; 31:23

Sadly, I don't think we hear the modern church fulfilling this scripture as it seeks to lead in the management of the surrounding culture:

Does not wisdom call, and understanding lift up her voice?
On top of the heights beside the way, where the paths meet,
she takes her stand; beside the gates, at the opening to the
city (Proverbs 8:1-3).

Our disengagement must stop now. The preservation of our nation and world depends upon the leaders of the Church getting back into our "city gates" and doing what moral leaders are supposed to do. "Give us justice and peace," we cry. Where can justice come from except from the Church? Justice cannot be expected to come from the unsaved and their immoral laws, which are often based on the lowest human standards of the powerful and degenerate. If the Church withholds its righteous leaders from the nation, the cities are doomed and the Church is held accountable. Let the liberators come! The release of the captives from the wicked await the government of God to set them free. As heaven's ambassadors, we can deny them our loving service?

Who Will Lead the Cities: The Church or the State?

In the final conflict of ideas, the two institutional antagonists we see are the Church and the secular state. The prize is the earth, and the instrument of victory is the allegiance of the people. The trench warfare will be fought in the nation's cities. Regional power is where it's at.

The secular state, through the Church's default, holds the upper hand right now. It has grown in direct proportion to the Church's withdrawal. It has sought, largely uncontested, to establish itself in the eyes of the people as the true shepherds and caretakers of their welfare. It has co-opted the Church and in many ways demanded to do the Church's true work. Why shouldn't it, since much of the Church withdrew from pastoring the nations? Some institution will lead and present itself as the guardian of mankind. In absentia, the Church can hardly complain if the top of the "city set on a hill" doesn't run Christ's flag, but the flag of the centralized secular power.

God's Duties for the Church to the Nations

We can no longer afford to shirk our duties. The fate of the world is at stake. The God-ordained duties of the Church to the nations and its cities are these:

1. To teach the people (Teacher)
2. To minister reconciliation to the people (Priest)
3. To instruct people in righteous law (Lawyer)
4. To help people understand how to create wealth, and care for the needy (Wealth Creator)

It is precisely these four offices (teacher, priest, lawyer and wealth creator) that the secular state has usurped. It contends that the Church should keep "the deal" and stay away from any ultimate role of power which surrounds these four functions. "Stay in the religious ghetto and leave the care of the land to the government. The Church should be seen and not heard, like a good boy," they patronizingly contend. It is these functions, and who exercises them, that will ultimately determine the fate of this planet.

The Church as Teacher

I will make you a light to the nations, so that my salvation may reach to the ends of the earth (Isaiah 49:6).
You are the light of the world (Matthew 5:14).
Go ye therefore and teach all nations (Matthew 28:19).

"The Church teach the nations?" says the humanist. "You must be kidding: the Church is politically irrelevant. The Church is dis-unified, the Church is hopelessly ignorant of the complexity of social and foreign policy issues and the Church is frequently prudish and simple-minded in its proposed solutions to complex problems."

The first thing the Church must do when confronted with the above charges, is plead guilty and repent. Have we fulfilled the Lord's description of us: "The children of this world are more shrewd in their generation than the children of light?" [5] Perhaps. But it is because of our own neglect and irresponsibility, not because of God's design. Get it straight: God has ordained us to teach the nations. The secular state has taken over because

[5] Luke 16:8

110

we have let it. We can stop this abuse of power right now by assuming the role God designed for us.

The second thing the Church must do is accept the enormous responsiblity of being the world's teacher and let that burden *mature* and *unify us.*

That they may all be one; even as Thou, Father, are in Me, and I in Thee, that they also may be in Us; that the world may believe that Thou didst send Me (John 17:21).

. . . and the Levites explained the law to the people. . . and they read from the book, from the law of God, translating to give the sense so the people understood the reading (Nehemiah 8:7,8).

It is wrong when the state assumes the position of evaluating and interpreting reality for all other human institutions. It is right when the Church assumes that position. The "people of the Book" must lead the nations as the world's priestly teacher. We cannot continue to allow the false prophets of the world system to force their ideology upon the nations.

The Apostle Paul says that he saw the great secret and mystery of God: the Church.[6] He saw the irreconcilable reconciled (the Jews and the Gentiles, formerly deadly enemies). He saw this new worldwide entity (the Church) ordained by God to be the teacher, healer, and steward of the kingdom of God, administering the mystery of God by the Spirit through the saints.

Paul saw in the Church's purposes what the Jews had been commissioned to do but had never clearly understood, to disciple the nations. "Disciple the nations and teach them to observe" is the Master's command to the Church. His love for the nations and the sure knowledge that they must be held accountable to God, demands that they have a rigorous teacher who will instruct them in the way they should go. In a democratic government, the job of the citizens of the kingdom is to get a majority of the voting populace to elect men and enact laws as much in line with biblical principles and covenants as is possible.

The humanists and the Marxists and those of other religions have sprinted for the teacher's chair. The Church was only too

[6] Ephesians 3:9-10

willing to give it up; it didn't want the responsibility. It wanted out of the pressures of the world, not wanting to be accountable to God for the world's condition. The consequence is that false Levites taught false laws and precepts to the people. The state, instead of the Church, has discipled the nations of the earth. We must organize to change that now.

The Church as Priest

The Church is also called to be the nation's priest. Peter called us "a nation of priests"[7] The Church should proclaim righteousness to individuals, but it should also proclaim righteousness to the nations.

As Priest to the people, the Church is God's instrument of reconciliation. We are to reconcile men to God, and man to man. It is the healing salve of forgiveness, compassion and truth that we are to gently knead into the wounds of our fellow man. We are called to do what the secular state with all its laws can never do:

> *The Spirit of the Lord God is upon me, because the Lord has anointed me—to bring good news to the afflicted; He has sent me to bind up the brokenhearted, to proclaim liberty to captives, and freedom to prisoners; to proclaim the favorable year of the Lord, and the day of vengeance of our God; to comfort all who mourn, to grant those who mourn in Zion, giving them a garland instead of ashes, the oil of gladness instead of mourning, the mantle of praise instead of a spirit of fainting. So they will be called oaks of righteousness, the planting of the Lord, that He may be glorified. Then they will rebuild the ancient ruins, they will raise up the former devastations, and they will repair the ruined cities, the desolations of many generations…But you will be called the priest of the Lord: you will be spoken of as ministers of our God. You will eat the wealth of nations, and in their riches you will boast (Isaiah 61:1-4,6).*

Who is anointed by God to do these wonderful things? The secular state? Never! It is Christ, the hope of glory through us.

---

[7] 1 Peter 2:9,10

It is the job of the Church, not the state, to turn the hearts of the rich to the poor, the man to his woman, the child to his parents and all men to their common Maker. May the healing oil of the Church flow like rivers through the streets of our cities.
The liberators are coming!

The Church must address whole nations and whole cities. Isaiah, Jeremiah, and Ezekiel are classic examples of men who spoke to the nations of the earth as judges and healers.

The Church as Healer

The secular state believes that it has the power not only to teach but also to heal. The cruelty of that misconception continues to grow. A classic case in point is what has happened in terms of black/white racial issues in the United States. Because most of the Church was asleep and preoccupied with other things when the Holy Spirit raised the issue of racism, only part of the Church—and that mostly black—responded. Who jumped in the gap as the purported reconciler and healer, claiming that it would resolve the problems legally and economically? The state. The phony doctor. God has not ordained it to be either teacher or healer.

Today the plight of the blacks in this country is still a disaster. The black family is virtually destroyed. The ghettos still remain, and the victories of the 60's for racial justice seem somehow hollow. Why? Because the state cannot heal. Only the gospel can heal, and only the Church, as society's priest, is anointed to do that. But to the Church's shame, it has been too preoccupied with "heavenly matters." It has not taught its pew sitters to be Christians committed to bring healing to the whole man.

The Church as Lawyer

The state is not free to establish its own laws independent from God without suffering the penalties of that disobedience. The world system wants to play God on the earth and set the laws for the people. It wants to define its own legal terms for "justice" and "freedom" apart from God's.

But God is the law-giver and the Church is His lawyer, empowered to represent His interests and edicts as His earthly real estate agent. The Church is to know God's laws so well that it can completely instruct the judicial, legislative and executive branches of our government on how to apply them to the growth, prosperity, and preservation of the nations.

The civil government cannot make men righteous because righteousness comes from within. What it must do, through the exhortation of the Church, is demand that righteous men run it. How many righteous men do you know in civil government today? Not many I suspect. It is the job of the citizens of the kingdom to make sure that righteous men are at the helm in civil government. A citizen of the kingdom recognizes that a pastor is no more important to God than a father is to the family, a righteous leader is to the civil government, or a God-ordained businessman is to commerce. They are all equally important in their own God-ordained spheres.

The civil government should guarantee its citizens peace and freedom from the fear of criminal violence. But because the secular state is against God's laws, it has made the criminal and moral deviant the object of its special protection. It makes sure that these law breakers' rights are protected at the expense of the safety of its citizens. Civil government is a moral reprobate whenever it protects criminals and creates an atmosphere of fear and anger among the general citizenry.

The government should establish a predictable legal framework where its citizens know that they will receive a fair and just hearing in the courts of law. "Justice and liberty for all" in this nation? Fat chance. Because the citizens of the kingdom have stayed in the Church instead of forcing these issues upon the state, they have guaranteed special care only for the criminal, the rich, and those who occasionally find it through sheer bureaucratic chance.

The Church as Family Protector

Under righteous law, the state should protect the family. It is to honor the covenant of marriage—since stable families are the cornerstone for stable nations—and to set its civil laws accordingly.

In honoring that covenant, its laws should establish and enforce the penalties for desertion and physical violence within the home.

Perhaps the greatest disservice secular government has done to the family is the unleasing of "no-fault" divorce laws. When this unbiblical standard was permitted in the United States in the 1960's, the flood of destruction to the family became incalculable. Half of the nations' marriages end in divorce and nearly half of the nation's children have no permanent family base from which to operate. Single parents are bound for life in a slum of substandard wages, family time, housing, social life, and family interaction. The Church is certainly culpable for this because the citizens of the kingdom did nothing about the "no-fault" divorce laws. They were too busy with their church meetings.

Prosperity Comes From the Family, Not the State

The secular state says that it has the power to bless the nations by creating wealth. The state says that if it hires lots of people to work for it, the nations will be wealthy and come out of poverty and bondage. It doesn't seem to bother itself with an ugly truth: the state can't create wealth, it can only transfer wealth that others have created through taxation. The state prints money that has no gold, silver, or real commodities behind it to back up the state's promise that the money is backed by value.

The Bible says that wealth for the nations comes out of the family unit:

> ...and in you [Abraham] all the families of the earth shall be blessed (Genesis 12:3).

Hard-working families create real wealth. That is why the secular state attacks the traditional family as a wealth-creator through promoting no-fault divorce, pornography, abortion, absentee-father welfare grants and oppressively high inheritance tax laws. The state in its more advanced socialist forms doesn't want families creating wealth; it wants to create phony wealth through its printing presses and increasing employment of its citizens.

The secular state hates Christians who say these things. But many of us have come to see that the emperor has no clothes. It can only tax the wealth from its hard working citizens. It spends your money and then tries to tell you, "the government is helping to meet the needs of the citizens by creating new jobs." Until the Church sees these truths clearly enough to change things, the debt accumulates and the family, as God's wealth creator, is weakened.

Of particular interest to the family in recent years is the state's ambivalence or lack of enforcement in four general areas: prostitution, pronography, drugs, and homosexuality.

These four tyrants have ravished the population by attacking the family unity. Pornography is an $8 billion a year industry taking in more revenues annually than the combined sales of the three major television networks. Child pornography grosses over half a billion dollars annually. It is impossible to estimate accurately the amount of money Americans are currently spending on drugs. And homosexuality, besides killing itself with self-induced disease, now threatens the general population with medical plagues of unknown proportions. Conservative estimates place AIDS deaths worldwide in the next five years at three to four million! The economic consequences of these attacks on the family are incalculable.

Calling Civil Government to God's Standards for Religious Freedom

The civil authority should guarantee religious freedom. This guarantee means that no man can be forced to believe a certain set of doctrines. The Church has been as guilty of religious tyranny at times in the past as any secular government. It is the responsibility of the civil government to protect society from denominational warfare. However, since all law is to be based on biblical principles, the state is convenantally held accountable to set biblically based laws which are not determined by any single denomination.

The civil government should make its plea to the Church for pastors and leaders to exhort their members to take up their civic responsibilities as functioning members of the kingdom of God. The Church should produce good citizens and the state should recruit them for its service.

God's Peace

For the joy of the Lord is my strength (Nehemiah 8:10). Whatever makes Jesus happy makes me strong. American Christianity is preoccupied with personal peace. Christians want to be "happy." Their focus is far too often on what Jesus can do for them rather than on how they can better serve Him. It is my deepest conviction that true joy only comes to those who are living their lives to please the Master.

The civil government, like all other institutions, should be preoccupied with serving the Lord in the public realm. If it does, its citizens will have a sense of personal joy because their government is creating for them a political atmosphere that is not only pleasing God but offering to its citizens the freedom to explore their own callings and destinies in the Lord. It should fulfill this scripture:

First of all, I urge that entreaties and prayers and petitions and thanksgivings be made on behalf of all men, for kings and all who are in authority, in order that we may lead a tranquil and quiet life in all godliness and dignity (1 Timothy 2:1-2).

If my government does not protect me physically from criminals, I can have neither peace nor joy. If my government does not protect me internationally I will be plagued by fears and anxieties over military invasion by enemies. If my government does not protect me commercially, I will not have the freedom to better myself and my family through personal effort and sacrifice. In short, the civil government should create an atmosphere of peace in the public realm analogous to the peace that the father is to supply to his family, the church leader is to supply in his local congregation, and the business leader is to supply in his commercial enterprise.

The state, under the Church's direction, should create an atmosphere where an individual, a family, or a business can build an estate in peace, knowing that no individual or governmental agency will rob from it the legitimate wages it has earned. The civil government ought to provide for its citizenry an atmosphere where they can take economic risks in peace. Property ought to be safe-guarded and access to jobs and employment fairly permitted.

Promoting Traditional Values

Evolutionism, Marxism, Fabian socialism, scientism, Freudianism, and the other "isms" are contributors to "new realities" which are just old illusions dressed up in new costumes. We have the New Nationalism (Teddy Roosevelt), the New Freedom (Woodrow Wilson), the New Deal (Franklin Roosevelt), and the New Frontier (John F. Kennedy). They all eventually ended up being bad "news."

We have seen all this before. It happened to the emperors of Rome after the year 200 AD. There was a string of them, each one announcing the dawn of a new era, and most of them dying violently. The Roman Empire was disintegrating, but each new emperor promised wonders. The "wonder" is why anyone in his right mind wanted to be emperor. And the answer is: hardly anyone in his right mind did. But there was no shortage of "wrong-minded" candidates.

We need a government under God which will reverse this dangerous deception and give us the traditional values which promote and protect individual rights, families, economic self-sufficiency, and social stability.

God's Rule Brings Hope for Our Cities

How are the nation's cities to be freed? Only through the renewal of men's characters and the resulting *transfer of authority to God's people*. If Christian rulership worries you, what could be worse than the death march most of the nations' major cities are now on as they endlessly pace around the prison floors of violence, smut, and poverty? Their leaders always come up with a new "answer" to get out of jail. But reality is that the chains are only getting tighter. And they will get tighter until the Church in each city begins to act as teacher, priest, judge, wealth-encouragers. When the Church leads the charge against hell's gates of oppression, they will fly open. Jesus promised. The liberators are coming!

So what, practically speaking, should we begin to do to serve the needs of our cities? The principle is simple although the programs and responses will be varied: church leaders and all Christians must ask themselves where *teaching* needs to take place in their city based on Biblical truth. They must ask, where is the ministry of *priestly* reconciliation needed? They must ask, how can they represent God's law as His lawyer and help bring justice through the enactment of Godly laws. And they must direct their energies towards the promotion of stability and prosperity through *support of the family.* When the Church begins to serve the cities by reclaiming its rightful role in these four ministries, we will indeed see the scripture fulfilled:

You will raise up the age-old foundations; you will be called the repairer of the breach, the restorer of the streets in which to dwell (Isaiah 58:12).

He who descended is Himself also He who ascended far above all the heavens, that He might fill all things.
(Ephesians 4:10)

CHAPTER NINE

There is Power in the Blood?

Do we believe that the power of sin in the world is greater than the power of Christ's cross? We extol the cross and sing the song, "There is power in the blood," but how much unbelief is in us as we sing? We trust God to save our sin-filled souls, but can we trust Him to massively impact nations? Why do Christians seem to believe that resurrection power can save our soul but it can't change our cities?

The Leaven of Sin or the Leaven of Righteousness?

He spoke another parable to them, The kingdom of heaven is like leaven, which a woman took, and hid in three pecks of meal, until it was all leavened (Matthew 13:33).

Jesus' kingdom will be revealed progressively on the earth. His power will eventually leaven the whole lump, the Bible says. That is the clear meaning of this parable. Jesus said that the kingdom *grows*, it doesn't just appear.

And He was saying, "The kingdom of God is like a man who casts his seed upon the ground; and goes to bed at night and gets up by day and the seed sprouts up and grows —how, he himself does not know. The earth produces crops by itself; first the blade, then the head, then the mature grain in the head. But when the crop permits, he immediately puts in the sickle because the harvest has come." And He said, "How shall we picture the kingdom of God, or by what parable shall we present it? It is like a mustard seed, which, when sown upon the ground, though it is smaller than all the seed that are sown upon the ground, yet when it is sown, grows up and becomes larger than all the garden plants and forms large branches; so that the birds of the air can nest under its shade" (Mark 4:28-32).

But if God's kingdom is to be revealed progressively, why isn't it the kingdom most clearly in evidence today? Why is the kingdom of secular humanism reigning right now? Because in our unbelief we have left the battlefield to the enemy while we retreated to our Christian ghettos, taking with us the power of the kingdom. Which kingdom's leaven is more powerful? Which yeast will make the loaf rise? Which is the dominant principle, corruption or incorruption? If we can't trust His blood to crush the serpent's head on the planet, how can we trust His blood to save our souls?

Too many Christians believe that the corruption principle is *more powerful than Christ*, even though He has risen from the dead. Although many Christians don't believe in the progressive manifestation of God's kingdom, they do believe in the progressive manifestation of Satan's kingdom! This means they believe God's leaven is weaker than Satan's, God's kingdom weaker than Satan's. If this is true, how can Jesus Christ be the "King of kings?"

No visible kingdom and no visible victory points to no serious king. But Christians worship a very serious king, a king who destroys the kingdoms of men repeatedly.[1]

The word "salve" comes from the same root as "salvation." Everything will be healed, bit by bit, by the gospel.[2] As this healing process continues, it makes manifest the kingdom of God. The Great Commission includes the gospel of the kingdom, the progressive manifestation of the kingdom on earth as well as in heaven. Jesus says his full authority is already operating.[3] Jesus said he had *all authority* on this earth 2000 years ago. The early Church acted like they believed His. We should too.

---

[1] Daniel 4:31-32 [2] Isaiah 9:6,7 [3] Matthew 28:18-20

We Must Have Kingdom Faith

God commands us to center our prayers on His kingdom coming to earth.[4] We must believe Jesus when He promises us that the leaven of faith will cause the kingdom to rise on the earth.

Our greatest challenge in this regard is faith. Too many Christians, like the doubting spies who checked out the Promised Land,[5] come back discouraged from surveying an earth filled with sin. We say in our hearts, "This cannot be the land of our inheritance. It is too sin-filled and men hate God. Our land must be heaven and the future." But our Lord reminds us of the good report of the two faithful spies, "It's a good land. It is My earth and I created it to be filled with My glory.[6] All power in heaven and on earth is given to me. I died on the cross to receive back the title deed to this world.[7] Go in My name and take the nations with the power of the gospel now!" But the giants of unbelief and the walled cities of earthly carnal power overshadow His cross. He said He had all authority, but we act as though His power is restricted to His Second Coming.

The early Church believed God's report, went with the power of the gospel, and battled Caesar and man-centered law for three centuries and won! Starting with nothing—except the Word of God and the Holy Spirit—they conquered the Roman Empire with the power of the gospel. Not all Roman citizens were converted, but most of them at last figured out that only the Church and its law could restore stability and some of Rome's lost prosperity.

We must believe God and act, in spite of the giants in the land. If the Marxists have taken most of the political globe in 60 years, what does that say about what we can do with God's blueprints for the nations if we only believe? It all centers on how we view the cross.

The Cross Is the Benchmark of All Human History

The cross of Christ and the work He did there, on behalf of God and man, is the single most important event in human history. Even Christ's entry into the world, as incredible as it was, is not

---

[4] Matthew 6:10 [5] Joshua 5:2-6 [6] Numbers 14:21; Psalm 46:10; Isaiah 6:3 [7] John 3:16

ultimately beneficial to man unless in His incarnation, sacrifice, and resurrection God rescued helpless man from his sin and death. And as glorious as will be His bodily return, it would mean little unless by His already-shed blood He has qualified us to be with Him in glory. The cross is the fulcrum for man. It alone levers him toward God's destiny for him. Theology that does not center in the victory of Christ's cross will eventually lead us into earthly despair and deception, as the Apostle Paul clearly warned the early Church:

See to it that no one takes you captive through philosophy and empty deception, according to the tradition of men, according to the elementary principles of the world, rather than according to Christ. For in Him all the fullness of Deity dwells in bodily form, and in Him you have been made complete, and He is the head over all rule and authority; and in Him you were also circumcised with a circumcision made without hands, in the removal of the body of the flesh by the circumcision of Christ; having been buried with Him in baptism, in which you were also raised up with Him through faith in the working of God, who raised Him from the dead. And when you were dead in your transgressions and the uncircumcision of your flesh, He made you alive together with Him, having forgiven us all our transgressions, having cancelled out the certificate of debt consisting of decrees against us and which was hostile to us; and He has taken it out of the way, having nailed it to the cross. When He had disarmed the rulers and authorities, He made a public display of them, having triumphed over them through Him (Colossians 2:8-15).

Don't let anyone take you into defeat by challenging the all-conquering power of what Christ won for man at His cross. Satan will always tell you (and well meaning Christians may tell you) that Christ's victory over sin on the earth was incomplete and needs His "finishing touches" at the second coming. Don't believe them! Christ's authority is already complete and we have been talked out of it only because of our unbelief. Paul told us that we are already complete in Him and he is "the head over all rule

126

and authority".[8] He is not waiting to do at His second advent what the Holy Spirit tells us that He *already did at his first.*[9] Jesus has already triumphed over the leaven of sin and crushed the serpent under His bruised heel at Calvary.

I know we don't have our resurrection bodies—the ordained plan is not completely executed yet—but we have a cross that has more power than man's fall and a Savior whose claim is already total on the governments of man. Christ is waiting for His people to come out of their unbelief and secular philosophies to believe *Him* when He says "all authority in heaven and on earth is Mine now, go ye therefore." If Jesus tells me that all earthly authority is now His, because of His blood-stained cross, I dare not call Him a confused Savior who tells me to go out and disciple nations that He doesn't own yet!

The Gospel Is the Victory of the Cross

At the cross Christ secured for believing man every blessed promise that obedience to the law guarantees. We all know the benefits of personal salvation and redemption which are ours individually through the cross, but there are corporate benefits of the cross, too. Let's look at an excellent section of the "good news" that Christ secured for us:

> *Now it shall be, if you will diligently obey the Lord your God, being careful to do all His commandments which I command you today, the Lord your God will set you high above all the nations of the earth. And all these blessings shall come upon you and overtake you, if you will obey the Lord your God. Blessed shall you be in the city, and blessed shall you be in the country. Blessed shall be the offspring of your body and the produce of your ground and the offspring of your beasts, the increase of your herd and the young of your flock. Blessed shall be your basket and your kneading bowl. Blessed shall you be when you come in, and blessed shall you be when you go out. The Lord will cause your enemies who rise up against you to be defeated before you; they shall come out against you one*

---

[8] Colossians 2:10 [9] Colossians 2:15

*way and shall flee before you seven ways. The Lord will
command the blessing upon you in your barns and in all
that you put your hand to, and He will bless you in the
land which the Lord your God gives you. The Lord will
establish you as a holy people to Himself, as He swore to
you, if you will keep the commandments of the Lord your
God, and walk in His ways. So all the peoples of the earth
shall see that you are called by the name of the Lord; and
they shall be afraid of you. And the Lord will make you
abound in prosperity, in the offspring of your body and in
the offspring of your beast and in the produce of your
ground, in the land which the Lord swore to your fathers
to give you. The Lord will open for you His good storehouse,
the heavens, to give rain to your land in its season and
to bless all the work of your hand; and you shall lend to
many nations, but you shall not borrow. And the Lord shall
make you the head and not the tail, and you only shall be
above, and you shall not be underneath, if you will listen
to the commandments of the Lord your God, which I charge
you today, to observe them carefully, and do not turn aside
from any of the words which I command you today, to the
right or to the left, to go after other gods to serve them*
(Deuteronomy 28:1-14).

What a set of blessings and promises Christ's obedience to God
secured on our behalf! Every promise of blessing is available to
us and every curse has been applied to His account. If we violate
God's laws, we will still suffer earthly penalties, but praise God
the death sentence is removed. In Christ's cross and resurrection
He has secured for man every life-giving blessing full obedience
to God guarantees.[10] This is incredible news! The powers that
held individuals and nations in the deadly coils of the serpent
were spoiled, nullified, and de-fanged at His cross. The head of
the serpent has been crushed and all we have to deal with now
is his scaly body thrashing around our legs, trying desperately
to convince us that this serpent still has authority over men and
nations. Raise your boot heel and see that squashed head.[11] Don't
condemn the nations to the imprisonment of waiting for a release

---

[10] 2 Corinthians 1:20   [11] Romans 16:20

at Christ's second coming that He has already secured for them at His cross.

The Right to God's Spirit

At the cross Christ's atoning blood gave us the unspeakable privilege of receiving the resurrection of life.[12] All the wisdom of the law is now ours as the Holy Spirit shows us how to interpret the law as the standard of all human conduct. "The letter kills, but the Spirit gives life."[13] Is God's law now inapplicable? No! The law was fulfilled in Christ, who has given us his Holy Spirit to instruct us in how to apply its life and blessings as Jesus did when he walked on the earth.[14] Now, through the power of the Spirit, we can begin to interpret for all men what it means for all men to live by "every word" that God has spoken. Now the structures of the world can be discipled to "obey whatsoever" He commanded. The cross secured the Holy Spirit for God's lawyer—the Church—to interpret as it affirms Christ's authority over the earth. Now we can, by God's Word and God's Spirit, believe to see a kingdom power of righteousness begin to make the loaf rise:

You are from God, little children, and have overcome them; because greater is He who is in you than he who is in the world (1 John 4:4).

Give The Bully What He Deserves

Improper theology has made the Church a coward, a victim of the earth's bully. Most of the Church acts as if the bully is going to chase the huddling Church off the earth in defeat. We are circling our wagons and waiting for a last minute rescue. We may have personal power but the leaven of international sin overpowers us from the world-system's attack. Instead of a triumphal entry into His kingdom, the Lord's appearing becomes a rescue mission for a people simply "hanging on till Jesus comes." Does your Bible teach you that the bully is still in control after Christ's cross? Mine doesn't.

---

[12] John 3:5 [13] 2 Corinthians 3:6,7 [14] John 14:16

129

My Bible teaches me that Christ is not coming to rescue a weak Church that sin chased off the earth but rather a glorious bride, without spot, blemish or wrinkle.[15] How will she get that clean? By standing up and letting the reality of Christ's victorious cross put the bully under Christ's feet! We are encouraged and exhorted: "The Lord will stretch forth Thy strong scepter from Zion, saying, 'Rule in the midst of Thine enemies.' "[16] The Bible says Christ is coming back to reign with the power of His cross.[17] "Let us rejoice and be glad and give the glory to Him, for the marriage of the Lamb has come and His bride has made herself ready" (Revelation 19:7).

When the bride (that's us, the Church) starts getting cleaned up, instead of beat up, we will be ready to meet him as He comes. Jesus is not coming for a pimply-faced, immature victim of a bully. He is coming after a companion that has been "kept from the evil one"[149] by learning how to dodge his deceptions while spoiling his goods! To the nations and the caring for people! The liberators are coming!

Accepting God's Purpose in the Midst of Paradox

Most people are uncomfortable with paradox, including Christians. We tend to want "either/or's" in life instead of the "both/and's".[19] We want one program or one doctrine that solves all problems, and we generally struggle with the contrasts we see around us that we think are irreconcilable.

Wheat and tares[20] in the same church drive most pastors crazy, but it is what Jesus promised them. To the mercy extender or Christian who demands total victory now, Jesus' statement, "the poor you have with you always"[21] is a source of incredible frustration. Immaturity drives us to deep distraction in the face of the paradoxes God allows. We want resolution, finality and completion, and we want it *now!* But total *completion* of the kingdom awaits His return. For now it is our lot to face victory in the midst of obstacles.

[15] Ephesians 5:27 [16] Psalm 110:2 [17] Acts 3:21 [18] John 17:15 [19] Acts 1:8 [20] Matthew 13:24-30
[21] Matthew 26:11

Christ's victorious cross has already judged Satan and restored all authority in heaven and earth to Christ. No nation now belongs to sin's power or is condemned to get more and more evil. If "Christ died for the sins of the whole world," it all belongs to Him. We were commanded to:

Arise, shine; for your light has come, and the glory of the Lord has risen upon you. For behold, darkness will cover the earth, and deep darkness the peoples; but the Lord will rise upon you, and His glory will appear upon you. And nations will come to your light, and kings to the brightness of your rising (Isaiah 60:1-3).

The scripture shows light and blessing on God's people and darkness and judgment on the disobedient. What did we see when God delivered his people from Egypt? We saw "light in Goshen but darkness in Egypt." What does Jesus tell us will accompany His second advent?

But all these things are merely the beginning of birthpangs. Then they will deliver you up to tribulation, and will kill you, and you will be hated by all nations on account of My name. And at that time many will fall away and will betray one another and hate one another. And many false prophets will arise, and will mislead many. And because lawlessness is increased, most people's love will grow cold. But the one who endures to the end, it is he who shall be saved. And this gospel of the kingdom shall be preached in the whole world for a witness to all the nations, and then the end shall come (Matthew 24:8-14).

We must learn to handle the birthpangs of Christ's kingdom *co-existing* with the death throes of the world's rebellion. The Church must suffer persecution even while it marches to victory. We are called to conflict in finding peace. We are peacemakers, yet a militant army. We are all imbued with the contrasting spirits of both a lion and a lamb.

Man wants everything in neat and tidy packages and God just won't play ball. We want Him to be the Prince of Peace,[22] without also being Him who came to bring division and a sword.[23] God

---

[22] Isaiah 9:6   [23] Matthew 10:34

works by attacking the problem from opposite sides at the same time. We want a neat and tidy view of prophecy and eschatology in which all Bible verses perfectly fit into our "system." We want it neat and tidy so we can walk by our prophecy charts and not by faith.[24] He may, before His second coming, give us such a neat package. But don't hold your breath. There may be at least as many surprises at His second coming as there were at His first. Our job is to occupy until He comes,[25] always being about the Father's business, letting Him sort out the final resolutions.

We can be sure about this: The cross is the key for victory. It alone gives us the power to fulfill this commandment: "Do not be overcome by evil, but overcome evil with good" (Romans 12:21). The cross removes not only our sin, but our excuses for not discipling the earth in his name. By God's grace, the liberators will do it.

---

[24] 2 Corinthians 5:7; Romans 8:25; 2 Corinthians 4:18   [25] Luke 19:13

. . . and they joined David. . . the sons of Issachar, men who understood the times, with knowledge of what Israel should do

(Chronicles 12:32)

CHAPTER TEN

Becoming Fishers of Men

The cry for relevancy is the heartbeat of all men and women who truly care. The supreme epitaph for a Christian ought to be: "He made a difference." Only the selfish simply want to go to heaven without helping free men, women, children, and nations first.

The Church must become relevant, heroic, and activist simply to survive the attacks upon it as the battle for the nations goes into the 1990's. Christians must either start catching masses of men and the agendas of our nations in our gospel nets[1] or be cemented in our ghettos by the secularists.

Relevant Caring

Relevancy comes through Spirit-led caring and effective action. As Christians become increasingly skilled in both, we can expect culture-wide evangelism on a scale not seen since the last "Great Awakening." The Word of God will become the topic of conversation in the secular media as Christian activism challenges the world for national power. This promotes worldwide revival, because faith comes by exposure to the Word of God,[2] and political involvement by the Church guarantees that God's Word will be the most talked-about subject of the day! The world will be forced to discuss our agenda.

Just caring is not enough. We must care about the issues that

---

[1] Matthew 4:19   [2] Romans 10:17

are defining the times, and not simply our own local church agendas. We must be as the men of Issachar, "who understood the times with knowledge of what Israel should do."[3] We must think globally (from the whole to the part), historically (where we are and why), and incrementally (from local to national).[4] When Christians do not think globally, they tend to miss the world mandate of "going to all the world." When Christians cannot identify the historical tides that shape and sweep their cultures, they cannot address the issues of the day. When Christians try to solve national problems without first solving neighborhood and city problems, they only reinforce the *centralizing of power*. We must recognize the truth that problems are best solved by those who locally are involved, or those who are qualified to solve large problems by virtue of their skill and training. Caring becomes effective by education and starting in our own backyards. When Nehemiah undertook the immense task of rebuilding Jerusalem's wall, he knew how to do it: the task was completed because the men built *locally*, that is, they built up the wall *in front of their own house*.[5]

Victorious Evangelism: Becoming Good Fishermen

Follow Me, and I will make you fishers of men.[6]

The Church must learn how to fish for men and nations. It must bait the hook of the gospel with answers to the questions that the *nations are asking* out of their need, instead of what we Christians want to feed them.

There is a great deal of difference between simply fishing and actually catching fish. I know. I have been fishing for nearly 40 years. Going through the motions with pole or net in hand won't bring in the fish if you don't know how to catch them. Many Christians simply go through the motions of evangelism because they've never learned how to bait their hooks with what people want, and they've never learned how to reel the line in after a bite without losing the catch.

---

[3] 1 Chronicles 12:32   [4] Luke 16:10   [5] Nehemiah 3:23,28,30   [6] Matthew 4:19

Fishing with the Right Bait

Jesus fished for men and women wherever He went, and He always used exactly the same bait or "evangelism program." He spoke to people's deepest needs. Whether it was their need for healing, deliverance, marriage counseling, finances, or forgiveness, Jesus always used the same methodology; what the "fish" was hungry for, was what He fed them.

Fishing is the analogy Jesus used to describe how He wants us to skillfully pull men and nations into His boat. As we go through ten basic elements of successful fishing, mentally check off what you or your church are or are not doing properly to bring souls and institutions into the kingdom.

1. *Go to the fish.* They won't come to you. "Come to my church on Sunday" is a far cry from taking the gospel truths out to where the fish are biting. Christ's command is "go" not "stay."

2. *Determine to catch fish, not take a nap in the sun.* Going through the motions of evangelism without committing yourself to saving souls and societies may make you feel good, but "witnessing" without catching fish is sleeping in the sun. A real fisherman catches real fish.

3. *Get the right equipment.* You cannot catch many fish without the right pole, the line, hook or lure, and the right bait. You have to know the water and something about the fish's feeding habits. To run off and evangelize without proper training, understanding of God's Word, and sensitivity to the needs of the world won't net you many converts.

4. *Find out what the fish are biting on.* Don't bring the wrong bait for the wrong pond. Christians love to talk to themselves in their own language instead of addressing people's needs in a language they can relate to. The fish are usually sick of our "Christianese."

5. *Hide the hook under the best bait.* The Bible says, "It is useless to spread the net in the eyes of any bird" (Proverbs 1:17). Isn't it amazing how foolish we Christians often are! We seldom cover our hook with care. Unlike the Apostle Paul, a skilled

fisherman who caught men with wisdom and cleverness,[7] we flash our hooks three blocks away.

6. *Be patient.* To fish is to wait. The water must be undisturbed and natural. In our retreat into our Christian ghettos we have become so different that we frequently stick out like a sore thumb when we venture out into the world. The world can't relate to us. We are unnatural instead of supernatural. Jesus was welcomed by the common man in the eating and drinking houses of His day,[8] a fact that would earn him a rebuke from many Christians I know if he weren't God!

7. *Land the fish once you've hooked it.* I don't know any fishermen who spend hours and hundreds of dollars hooking fish and then sit there and watch them get away because they don't know how to land them. And yet I know plenty of Christians who get somebody all hooked on the gospel but never bring them to a decision for Christ. People must be taken to a point of decision. The deal must be closed.[9]

8. *Let God sort out the ''keepers'' and release the others.* The job of discerning between keepers and throw-away's is not technically ours, it belongs to the Holy Spirit.[10] But don't sidetrack your whole evangelism program for individuals and nations because of isolated "failures."

9. *Get the fish cleaned.* People need to be cleansed from sin before they can be of full service to the king. Be sure your "fish" are in a good discipleship program before you let go of them.

10. *Use the fish.* It's a waste to catch fish just to have them rot on the dock. Good fishermen see that their whole catch is used. Unused lives are the tragedy of our age. All Christians must be employed in the Lord's ministry. A New Testament church is one where the number saved equals the number serving. Ultimate evangelism is hiring people into God's purposes for their lives.[11]

For all its value as an analogy, fishing is trivial compared to the incomparable worth of a soul or nation redeemed from the fire through Spirit-anointed evangelism. As the Church cooperates

[7] 1 Corinthians 9:22 [8] Matthew 9:10,11; 11:19; Mark 2:16; Luke 7:34 [9] Matthew 12:30 [10] Matthew 13:47,48 [11] Matthew 20:1,7

in both personal and cultural evangelism with the convicting power of the Holy Spirit, we will see revival, national repentance, and spiritual and material prosperity beyond anything we can even imagine.

Evangelism in the Footsteps of the Lord

> *Your own wickedness will correct you, and your apostasies will reprove you; know therefore and see that it is evil and bitter for you to forsake the Lord your God, and the dread of Me is not in you,"* declares the Lord God of hosts (Jeremiah 2:19).

God uses men's own sins to break their hard hearts toward Him. The wounds of a nation prepare it for the seed of God's Word. God is thereby able to make even sin serve His purposes,[12] and its greatest service is to create desperate hunger for relief from broken lives and seemingly unsolvable personal and national problems. Disobedience makes the people hungry. Our job is to perceive their needs and feed them relief. "For when the earth experiences Thy judgments, the inhabitants of the world learn righteousness" (Isaiah 26:9).

God wants to raise a standard for the nations through His Church.[13] He wants to heal nations by bringing down their false gods and unjust institutions, giving them the life found in His Word.

In order to accomplish all of this, God must first plow up the nations. His "judgment plow" must open the soil for His Word by humbling them and making them receptive for the seed. Most of the plowing is already being done by the laws of sowing and reaping.[14]

So the Lord need not lean too heavily on the blade. The back of the backslider is already split in agony through self-induced affliction. The harvest of disobedience is preparing the nations for the liberators.

[12] Genesis 50:20   [13] Isaiah 60:1-4   [14] Galatians 6:7

Issuing A Call For Prophetic Evangelism

Most of what we currently call "evangelism" is designed to lead individuals to Christ and then to pastor them. Prophetic evangelism, on the other hand, is the preaching of Christ's Word to whole cultures. Prophetic evangelism is the focus of this book and the central concern of Christian activism. The prophetic work of the Church challenges the whole culture and its political institutions to conform to the principles of God's Word.

Today's media, newspapers, films, and news broadcasts are the chronicles of where and how God is preparing the nations for his Word by plowing up their soil. When I read them I see what God is doing to prepare the people of the earth for His great coming revival. They show us the rupturing and hemorrhaging of entire value systems and economic orders. The deeper the problems they reveal, the softer the hearts of the people are becoming to God's Word. The plow is doing its work.

Prophetic evangelism follows the pre-evangelism God uses to wound the nations with their sin, making them so sick of their own unrighteousness that they willingly embrace the gospel when we follow up with it. What God has chosen to make an issue of through pain and need in a nation is designed to get that society to ask questions in these areas. The Church's job is to help the nations see what the real issues are and then give them the right answers.

Righteousness and justice are the foundations of Thy throne; loving kindness and truth go before Thee. How blessed are the people who know the blessed sound! O Lord, they walk in the light of Thy countenance. In Thy name they rejoice all the day (Psalm 89:14-16).

How can we "rejoice all the day long" when things are falling apart? The people of God rejoice that unrighteousness is preparing the hearts of the wounded world to respond to the healing gospel. Christian politics is the healing art of salting the wounds of society's broken institutions in such a way as to turn them from their sins and avoid the Master's judgment in the future.

Setting The Hook When The Right Questions Are Asked

Now when they heard this, they were pierced to the heart, and said to Peter and the rest of the apostles, "Brethren, what shall we do?" (Acts 2:37).

To the fisher of men the sweetest sound in the world is, "What must I do?" The bait has been taken because the need has been identified, and now the hook must be set in their jaws. Our "setting of the hook," in the principles of this book, is the church's seizing of the agenda of our cities through the operation of the four loving ministries of the Church.

In Chapter Eight we read about seizing our cities and nations' agendas as the Church recognizes and acts out its four offices as teacher, priest, lawyer and wealth-stimulator. Now I can say what you didn't have the foundation to understand then: these same four roles are the four fishing hooks we use for the bait of the gospel for which God has prepared the nations.

The Church as Teacher. The Church offers reality so that, when people ask what to do, we can free them and heal them with truth. The Church, not the world system, has the real answers to the question. The world system has made them sick. We can point them to the Great Physician.

The Church as Priest. The Church offers reconciliation to the human race as it tears itself apart. Man against man, race against race, male against female, parent against child, and man against himself provides an incredible fishing pond. The Priest comes with healing that looks like bait.

The Church as Lawyer. The Church offers righteousness and justice as it seeks to persuade men that God's laws are not unfair and cruel.[15] The laws of secularism produce the politics of death, division, and unreality. Our fishing hooks carry with them genuine possibilities for order with freedom.

The Church as Wealth—Stimulator. Through the healthy family unit, the Church offers prosperity to the world. Poverty is a result of sin—both personal and in the world at large. Prosperity that lasts[16] is almost always created from healing shuttered family units.

---

[15] 1 John 5:3.   [16] Proverbs 13:11

Hunger and privation ought not only to move the Church to respond, it ought to reinforce the Church's ability to show others how to create wealth and meet human needs. The "lips of the righteous feed many" (Proverbs 10:21).

The Church Balanced in Evangelism and Prophecy

Over the last 300 years, the Church has been unbalanced. We have evangelized and led millions of people to a saving knowledge of Christ, the value of which is beyond measure. But we're still unbalanced. We haven't been the evangelistic Church and the prophetic Church. If both these thrusts were focused from the Church into the world, the world would be turned upside down by the kingdom. Instead, we act as though personal evangelism is all there is to our responsibility to the nations of the earth. While we've brought a saving word to men who were dying spiritually, we've neglected to bring salvation and redemption to the world's social processes.

The Church is evangelistic when it reaches out to individual men, but it becomes *prophetic* when it acts as salt and light to the culture that surrounds it. Never before in our history have the nations needed a prophetic Church more. We have been living off of the stored up spiritual capital and blessings of previous generations. If we fail to address our culture's social bankruptcy, we will miss the greatest opportunity for cultural revival in centuries. The American people are ready for the Church to speak prophetically.

The prophets of old called their own nations and surrounding nations to biblical obedience, seeking to save souls while addressing the social fabric of the entire nation. When Jonah went to Nineveh, more than 40,000 people repented in response to the prophetic Word. For the Church not to address our cities, torn with sin and institutional injustice, is to rob millions of people of the blessings and regeneration of the whole Word of God.

God asks, "Who will stand up for Me against evildoers? Who will take his stand for Me against those who do wickedness?" (Psalm 94:16). Are we so busy in our meetings and in our individual soul-winning that we do not care for those slaughtered in the streets? Does the parable of the Good Samaritan[17] have any application to the nations of the world? Are nations permitted to watch idly as other nations are beaten and left for dead along the international highways of the earth and go unchallenged? If the earth is the Lord's, doesn't He have standards of global concern for the protection of the weak?

True power does not come from the barrel of a gun. It comes from the Lord. Take the challenge. Shoulder your responsibility as a Christian. Bring salvation to the nations as well as to individuals! The liberators are advancing, with fishing poles in hand! Ezekiel saw us coming:

And it will come about that every living creature which swarms in every place where the river goes will live. And there will be very many fish, for these waters go there, and the others become fresh; so everything will live where the river goes....And it will come about that fishermen will stand beside it (Ezekiel 47:9,10).

---

[17] Luke 10:30-37

"Yet once more I will shake not only the earth, but also the heaven." *And this expression,* *"Yet once more,"* *denotes the removing of those things which can be shaken, as of created things, in order that those things which cannot be shaken may remain. Therefore, since we receive a kingdom which cannot be shaken, let us show gratitude, by which we may offer to God an acceptable service with reverence and awe*

(Hebrews 12:26-28)

CHAPTER ELEVEN

Getting Ready To Rule In A World Falling Apart

C hristians should go out into the world and do far more than simply evangelize: they should be preparing to rule. It is their destiny.[1] The choice is not to evangelize or to take dominion. No such biblical choice exists. We must do both. We must win souls and we must let God establish his order through us. In both cases we are ruling, either finding the lost sheep and bringing it back into the fold, or administrating the prosperity of the whole flock and the Master's land.

Deceived by a False Heaven

Few deceptions have undermined the Church's commitment to rule on earth as much as the strange notions many Christians have led us to believe about our future in heaven. Heaven, and the saints' ultimate calling, has been portrayed as anything but what Jesus said it was. We have been told that eternity will be spent lying around on clouds, playing harps. When we tire of that we'll put on our golden slippers, walk around the North Gate, go to our little cabins, and sit down to rock in our rockers. In short, heaven is freedom from work and responsibility. Heaven is the ultimate weekend!

[1] Revelation 3:21

This *anti-work* attitude shows us something about many Christians' real values, doesn't it? They have been deceived into believing that playing or doing nothing is our ultimate destiny. Imagine how silly and yet tragic this lie must seem to our God who, Jesus said, "is always working."[2]

There is nothing very silly or funny about this lazy man's "paradise" concept at all. It is a demonic lie that has paralyzed millions of Christians into believing that work, responsibility, and ruling is an earthly curse which heaven removes. What is the net effect of this lie? It is two-fold:

First, Christians have forsaken taking dominion through working on the earth. Second, they have made heaven and lazy stupor their ultimate goal instead of maturity and co-ruling with Christ.[3] How you see your heaven is how you plan your life. The saints haven't ruled on earth because they came to believe work was a temporary evil which heaven would remove.

Christians' ultimate destination is not that kind of heaven. It is a renewed heavens and earth.[4] The earth is the center of God's focus and creation.[5] Jesus is coming back *to the earth* to dwell forever and so is His bride, the Church.[6] So central to Christ is the earth that His prayer instructions focused on it: "Thy kingdom come. Thy will be done, on earth as it is in heaven" (Matthew 6:10). Our calling on earth is to rule cities and nations.[7] Our current training is to be the source of our future work:[8]

And the Lord said, "Who then is the faithful and sensible steward, whom his master will put in charge of his servants, to give them their rations at the proper time? Blessed is that slave whom his master finds so doing when he comes. Truly I say to you, that he will put him in charge of all his possessions (Luke 12:42-44).

Occupying Till He Comes
And while they were listening to these things, He went on to tell a parable, because He was near Jerusalem, and they

---

[2] John 5:17 [3] Romans 8:17 [4] Revelation 21:1-3, 22-26; Zechariah 14:5-9 [5] Genesis 1:14-17 [6] Revelation 21:10 [7] Luke 19:17 [8] Matthew 24:45-47

*supposed that the kingdom of God was going to appear im-
mediately. He said therefore, ''A certain nobleman went
to a distant country to receive a kingdom for himself, and
then return. And he called ten of his slaves, and gave them
ten minas, and said to them, 'Do business with this until
I come back.' But his citizens hated him, and sent a delega-
tion after him, saying, 'We do not want this man to reign
over us.' And it came about that when he returned, after
receiving the kingdom, he ordered that these slaves, to
whom he had given the money, be called to him in order
that he might know what business they had done. And the
first appeared, saying, 'Master, your mina has made ten
minas more.' And he said to him, 'Well done, good slave,
because you have been faithful in a very little thing, be in
authority over ten cities.' And the second came, saying,
'Your mina, master, has made five minas.' And he said
to him also, 'And you are to be over five cities.' And another
came, saying, 'Master, behold your mina, which I kept put
away in a handkerchief; for I was afraid of you, because
you are an exacting man; you take up what you did not
lay down, and reap what you did not sow.' He said to him,
'By your own words I will judge you, you worthless slave.
Did you know that I am an exacting man, taking up what
I did not lay down, and reaping what I did not sow? Then
why did you not put the money in the bank, and having
come, I would have collected it with interest?' And he said
to the bystanders, 'Taken the mina away from him, and
give it to the one who has the ten minas.' And they said to
him, 'Master, he has ten minas already.' 'I tell you, that
to everyone who has shall more be given, but from the one
who does not have, even what he does have shall be taken
away. But these enemies of mine, who did not want me to
reign over them, bring them here, and slay them in my
presence' ''* (Luke 19:11-27).

This parable is rich in instruction for us who are to be "taking
care of business" until He comes again.

1. *Stewardship of God's possessions.* The entire parable is about caring properly for the king's property. Those who multiplied the assets they supervised were rewarded. Those who hid the assets away and refused to develop them were stripped of even that little position of leadership.

2. *Rewards of leadership.* Jesus tells us that we are in training for responsible leadership positions, not for cloud hopping. We are being trained to administrate cities. Political involvement is an earthly responsibility as well as a *heavenly* calling.

3. *Results of obedience.* Jesus affirmed that He expects increase on His investments. This is echoed in John 15:1,2, where He says, "I am the true vine, and My Father is the vinedresser. Every branch in Me that does not bear fruit, He takes away; and every branch that bears fruit, He prunes it, that it may bear more fruit."

To win souls without extending and increasing God's rule on His planet belies our loyalty to the king. The servant who jealously refused to produce fruit for his king was stripped of his possessions.

Healing the Nations As They Fall

Christians are called to heal the nations and to serve them even after the Lord's return. Nations are a unit that will pass into the next eon of time and will continue to be the object of God's work.

And he showed me a river of the water of life, clear as crystal, coming from the throne of God and of the Lamb, in the middle of its street. And on either side was the tree of life, bearing twelve kinds of fruit, yielding its fruit every month; and the leaves of the trees were for the healing of the nations (Revelation 22:1-2).

But prior to the Lord's return, the nations will collapse and fall toward our hands. The secularists have built them upon faulty and false foundations. Everything which is not built upon the foundation of the law of God is will be destroyed. Nothing else has either the right or the strength to stand. As nations do fall, the Church is supposed to catch them. They are our inheritance.

GETTING READY TO RULE

The Prophet Haggai saw the nations falling into the Church's care thousands of years ago:

And I will shake all the nations; and they will come with the wealth of all nations; and I will fill this house with glory, says the Lord of hosts (Haggai 2:7-9).

Upheaval and bankruptcy are the lot of those whose lives are not built upon the rock of God's truth.[9]

To whatever degree a nation is rebellious to the commandments of God, that disobedience determines the amount of debris which must fall upon its head. As the end of this age approaches, the eternal values of God will increasingly expose and challenge the sandcastle reality of men.

Because God loves man, He always provides him with a safety net in which to fall when his sins overcome him. That net is available, but only to those who will accept it. To the unrepentant, even the net's bottom falls out. The *Church* is God's safety net for the falling nations that will repent; they are to fall into God's loving arms through us.

As God's provision for the nations, the Church's readiness and ability to heal the fallen institutions is God's timetable for judgment and upheaval. God will not destroy without first providing warning, a plan, and a place of healing. To the nations of the earth, the Church is designed to be both. We are asked to be the witness of God to the nations and we are created to be the place where God's plan and place of healing binds up their wounds. God, because He is love, only tears down with one hand what He can catch with the other. And the Church is designed to be the hand of God upon the earth.

With the Church as God's safety net, ultimate spiritual warfare can best be described as Satan's attempt to tear down the nations of the earth *faster than the Church can deal with their debris*. It is the work of the Holy Spirit to monitor the rate of God's judgment, so that the nations of the earth do not come apart faster than God's hospital (the Church) can cleanse the wounds and instruct the nations in the way that they should go. Those in the Church who teach that our job is to get people

[9] Matthew 7:24-27

151

saved and to get them out of here as fast as we can do not understand the love and compassion of God for the nations of the earth.

Eventually, we will leave the earth, but not until every nation and every tongue has had the privilege of hearing and seeing, by the Church's example, how they should live to prosper in every aspect of their lives.

Getting Bad To Get Better

God is in the process of letting the nations get deathly ill. A doctor has little value unless you are sick. The sicker the nations get, the more receptive they will become to the message of the Great Physician. Their cries and despair are the pre-birth symptoms that the Church—the Physicians midwife—is looking for. This process of emphasizing the negative, so that when the positive arrives it is acutely desired, is what I call "framing."

Framing is a tool God uses to reveal the true depth of human need. You don't know how sick you really are until someone who is radiantly healthy is paraded in front of you. It was the splendor of Jesus' spiritual condition that revealed the true sickness of the religious leaders of his day.

God wants to frame the richness and health of His kingdom, expressed through the Church against the contrast of the dirty, decayed edging of bankrupt, sick nations. The rebellious nations' diseases must come to full term.[10] When the nations are desperate enough, they will clearly see the redemption mirrored in the Church and in Christian politics and will flock to salvation. Isaiah shows us this "framing" principle clearly in the following text:

Arise, shine; for your light has come, and the glory of the Lord has risen upon you. For behold, darkness will cover the earth, and deep darkness the peoples; but the Lord will arise upon you, and His glory will appear upon you. And nations will come to your light, and kings to brightness of your rising. Lift up your eyes round about, and see; they all gather together, they come to you. (Isaiah 60:1-4).

---
[10] Revelation 18:2-5

Many will "inquire of the Lord" in that day and we had better have done our homework. If those smashed nations come to the Church for answers and we only give them religious slogans, may God have mercy on the Church! As Isaiah says once again of the nations' journey toward God:

Thus says the Lord God, "Behold, I will lift up My hand to the nations, and set up My standard to the peoples; and they will bring your sons in their bosom, and your daughters will be carried on their shoulders" (Isaiah 49:22).

God expects the Church to grow spiritual food and develop spiritual leadership for the nations as they descend into their self-induced famines and anarchy. Their disobedience will starve many of them into submission to God's message. Bankrupt and hungry men will usually listen to a message if they are convinced you have something tangibly valuable and nourishing. Our job is to draw the food from God's Word and store it up for application as the Lord judges the nations. The Church is God's corporate Joseph, sent before the famine, to store up life for the people of the earth.

Disaster Is Coming

What an incredible experience it is to watch God's Spirit racing[11] to prepare the Church for her leadership role as the world tumbles at increasing speed into disaster. At this very hour there are at least eight or nine major world problems, any one of which could bring the world into some kind of massive crisis beyond anything the modern world has ever seen. Here are just five of the imminent crises God may use to turn the nations upside down.

1. *The Debt Crisis*

The love of money is the root of all sorts of evil (1 Timothy 6:10).

If thou lend money to any of my people that is poor by thee, thou shalt not be to him as a usurer, neither shalt thou lay upon him usury (Exodus 22:25). Take no usury of him, or increase...thou shalt not give him thy money upon usury (Leviticus 25:36-37).

---

[11] Revelation 22:7

Unto thy brother thou shalt not lend upon usury: That the Lord thy God may bless thee (Deuteronomy 23:20).

In the early Church, any interest on debt was considered usury, and was a crime. Compound interest is often called the "eighth wonder of the world," since it multiplies the principal debt at such an incredible rate. America—indeed the whole world—is now facing a virtually unsolvable debt crisis, due to overspending and the interest rates attached to that debt.

In 1901 the national debt of the United States was less than $1 billion. It stayed at less than $1 billion until World War I, then it jumped to $25 billion.

Between 1918 and 1942, on the eve of America's entry into World War II, the national debt almost doubled - from $25 to $49 billion.

Between 1942 and 1952, the debt rose from $72 billion to $265 billion. In 1962 it was $303 billion. Only eight years later, in 1970, it was $383 billion.

Between 1971 and 1976 it rose from $409 billion to $631 billion. By the end of 1986, government debt reached over $2 trillion. It had taken 206 years to reach one trillion dollars in government debt, and only five more years to double it to two trillion. From 1975 through 1986, Federal debt quadrupled. The U.S. is now the largest debtor nation in the world, the first time we've had that distinction in 71 years.

How much interest are we paying for the "privilege" of spending our great-grandchildren's inheritance, deserting the principle of generational thinking? Within the next year more than 25% of the U.S. budget is for interest payments alone! Within five years, it will be around 40%. Remember, this is *interest only*, with no attempt to repay any amount on the principal. In order to cover our current national debt, every man, woman, and child in America today now owes nearly two thousand dollars to future generations. This is on top of the nearly 40% tax load most Americans pay already on current income, when all hidden taxes are counted.

As a point of comparison, the Revolutionary Colonists went to war with England over a tea tax surcharge of less than 2%! As more and more paper money is needed to "print over" this huge debt chasm, expect inflation to go back into high gear.

What about private and corporate debt? U.S. corporate debt is growing at an unprecedented 15% per year. America's largest corporations' liquidity is dropping at incredible rates. Total *consumer debt* grew over the last dozen years from $750 billion to nearly $3 trillion—a triple increase. Its current growth rate is at about 20% at an annual rate. As a result of these staggering figures, a landslide of private and corporate bankruptcies has emerged. More than 1200 banks (one out of twelve in the nation) are on the FDIC's problem list. This figure is up almost 500% from the 250 banks in 1983. The Savings and Loans are in much worse shape yet—but I'll spare you.

What about global debt? Global debt is exploding as well. Soviet bloc, third world nations and Latin debts now total over $1.2 trillion. Other oil-related debt is over $1 trillion, with domestic oil companies' debt at about $250 billion. The collapsing prices of oil have done incredible damage to the world debt problem since major third-world oil-producing countries look to their oil sales to accumulate revenues to service their debts.

Latin America owes U.S. banks billions of dollars a year in interest payments alone. Mexico and other debtor nations, directly affected by fallen oil prices as either sellers or buyers, have had catastrophic shocks to their ability to repay U.S. backed back loans. Default is a real issue at worst, with interest-only repayments at best a real possibility. What will this do to the U.S. banking industry? You can guess, but you won't like the answer. The nations of the earth could be in the initial stages of a fatal financial disease.

2. *The Employment Crisis*

All this debt will force loan defaults, inflation, world trade crisis, and massive unemployment as the economies of the world try to readjust. Ultimately, it will all come tumbling down. Last year's

U.S. balance of trade deficit came near the $200 billion mark. Domestic workers are threatened in every sector from foreign products and services. Nearly 300 protectionist bills in Congress were introduced to try and plug the hole. The sign of the time is clear; trade war is brewing.

How will this affect employment? Our Federal government will not be able remain the nation's biggest employer; print money (inflate the economy); keep institutional partnerships intact during a trade war; and prop up falling banks, savings and loans, and defaulted debtor nations.

Right now our Federal government accounts for over 25% of all U.S. economic activity, owns over 740 million acres of land, employs nearly 5 million people, and runs over 960 subsidized programs at an annual cost of more than $400 billion while providing medical care for 47 million people. No sane man can really believe this will stay intact when God starts allowing nations to fall into the dire consequences of their own monetary and fiscal sins.

3. *The National Defense Crisis*

The geopolitics of this hour is worse than ever. The Middle East is convulsed by the Iran/Iraq War, fueled by the rise of a militant Islam faith. World oil supply is the bottom line, and now all major powers are jockeying for position. The Soviets promote terrorism and destabilization through Syria and Libya, while Israel's existence is still threatened by many. There are eight counter-revolutionary wars being waged around the world challenging the so-called "Brezhnev Doctrine," by which the Soviets mean that once a nation becomes Marxist, the Soviets will never permit it to change its mind. Central America and Mexico have unstable, deteriorating governments and economies that are ripe for violent, revolutionary overthrow. The multi-faceted crises in South Africa potentially threaten free world mineral and defense supplies.

The Soviets continue to expand the greatest military machine in world history, increasing their leads over the United States in virtually every area. Extremist elements in all nations are polarizing. How do you think this volatile foundation will fare in the shaking?

4. *The Entitlements Crisis*

When the debt bomb explodes, and employment falls, triggering devastating inflation, the social security system will be a cruel joke. Through abortion this nation has already killed off 20 million babies, 20 million potential wage earners to buttress the entitlement system. In killing off the unborn, our murder has condemned the aged and the poor of our society as well.

The system cannot sustain the blows of (1) increased retirement costs on fixed income against inflated dollars, (2) increased percentage of retired workers against a relative decrease in the number of supporting full-time workers, (3) sky-rocketing health-care costs. Think about this. The number of AIDS patients in 1992 is projected conservatively to be 225,000 Americans. In 1986 dollars, it will cost nearly $175,000 to care for each one from diagnosis to certain death. This amounts to over $39 billion dollars in a single year alone. Do you have any guesses as to what this will do to our hospitals, medical staffs, insurance companies and national health care funds? Will there be anything left for the care of the poor, the jobless, and the homeless?

5. *The Family Crisis*

The male-female wars, the parent-child wars, and the monogamy-promiscuity wars have been quietly causing our whole western culture to teeter for the last fifteen years. The "do your own thing" rebellion, in its quest for something to fill up the huge hole which the removal of God's values left in our culture, has destroyed nearly 50% of this generation's families. The cost relationally, morally, and economically is beyond description.

Let's Get Ready

Are we going to be ready to rescue the falling lives and falling nations? I *know* we're not ready right now, but we must begin today to change our lives, our families, and our churches into the image of Christ to fill His shoes as His caretakers until His coming. We have no time to lose. When everything collapses, the Church must be prepared to rule with justice, compassion, and wisdom born of maturity. Hear the Word of the Lord: And they sang a new song, saying,

> *Worthy art thou to take the book, and to break its seals; for Thou wast slain, and didst purchase for God with Thy blood men from every tribe and tongue and people and nation. And Thou hast made them to be a kingdom and priests to our God; and they will reign upon the earth* (Revelation 5:9,10).

May we get in shape quickly so that our skill in caring and ruling meets the needs of the damaged masses!

RISE UP O MEN OF GOD

Rise up O men of God!
Have done with lesser things;
Give heart and soul and mind and strength
To serve the King of Kings.

Rise up O men of God!
His kingdom tarries long;
Bring in the day of brotherhood,
And end the night of wrong.

Rise up O men of God!
The Church for you doth wait:
Her strength unequaled to her task;
Rise up and make her great!

Lift high the cross of Christ!
Tread where His feet have trod;
Brothers of the Son of Man
Rise up O men of God!

(William Pierson Merrill, 1867-1954). †

† *Used by permission of* The Presbyterian Outlook, *Richmond, VA (USA)*

CHAPTER TWELVE

Calling For Christian Heroes

The systems of this world are dying. Their ability to motivate men to action has passed. Globally, our kingdom hasn't begun to brightly shine. It won't until we "rise up" and be done with fear and Christian ghettos. And yet even the world system is now turning to spiritual and religious modes to deal with their morally deflated cultures.

Socialists and Marxists turn to "liberation theology," Satan's ultimate false marriage of Christiantiy and social engineering. It is a deadly enemy of the true Church because it attempts to "christianize" the politics of violent and revolutionary exploitation, denying personal redemption and national liberation in the regenerative power of Jesus Christ.

Marxism has run out of moral fuel — the ability to call people up to sacrifice out of moral conviction. Instead it must rely on fear, love of power, or simply going along with the path of least resistance. This event was long ago foreseen by the Soviet's founder, V. I. Lenin. His well-known quote is now being fulfilled in liberation theology:

We shall find our most fertile field for the infiltration of Marxism within the field of religion, because religious people are the most gullible and believe almost anything as long as it is clothed in religious language.

However well-intentioned some liberation theologians are in their genuine concern for the exploitation of the poor, their "answer" is but another poison. Self-government and self-determination must be our ultimate goal for political systems. Marxism offers a universally marginal lifestyle in exchange for a grotesquely authoritarian, permanent dictatorship. The answer to exploitation is service, and it cannot be externally enforced through the theft of private property, presided over by a dictatorial central government. Liberty is an affair of the heart.

The liberal establishment even recognizes now that society cannot hold together without the moral fuel of religion to empower it. A 1985 report published by the Brookings Institution — one of the country's largest and most prestigious organizations of scholarly research — concluded that the stability and future strength of American democracy depends on her religious foundations. Without it, "democracy lacks essential moral support" to sustain it, says the report. It is interesting to note that Brookings has long been regarded as *liberal* in its appraisals. After three years analyzing the basic ingredients that hold society together, the author concluded that secular value systems failed "to meet the test of intellectual credibility" for doing the job.

"Representative government depends for its health on values that over the not-so-long run must come from religion," the report says. "A society that excludes religion totally from its public life, that seems to regard religion as something against which public life must be protected, is bound to foster the impression that religion is either irrelevant or harmful." Persons subscribing to a classical humanist ethic "are driven to hypocrisy or cynicism," the report continues, either pretending a "fellow feeling for the masses: not sustained by that value system, or scorning their ways." "In either case, social bitterness between humanist elites and "the mass of working-class and middle-class citizens is bound to follow."[1]

Religion will increase. But will it be secularized Christianity, having a "form of Godliness but denying the power thereof" (2 Timothy 3:5), or will it be kingdom Christianity, coming with the power and redemption of Jesus Christ? This rhetorically motivating question was also asked by Jesus:

---

[1] A. James Reichley. *Religion in American Public Life*. Washington DC: The Brookings Institution. 1985.

However, when the son of Man comes, will He find faith on the earth? (Luke 18:8)

Working Realistically For The Long Haul

The Christian Liberator doesn't expect a perfect earth or an easy or quick victory. He knows that sin and imperfection will be with us until the Lord Himself.[2] He is looking for a world that is experiencing more and more freedom in the midst of the world's corruption. There is no way back into the Garden, but there is a way that leads to liberty. Jesus promises, "you shall know the truth and the truth shall make you free" (John 8:32).

The Christian Liberator asks, "How do I act most effectively and to whom should I give my time, energy and resources?" Out of this heart cry comes a Christianity whose witness and effectiveness will rebuke and overshadow the sham religions which either exist now, or are waiting to appear.

The Power of Living For Others

Therefore, since we have so great a cloud of witnesses surrounding us, let us also lay aside every encumbrance, and the sin which so easily entangles us, and let us run with endurance the race that is set before us, fixing our eyes on Jesus the author and perfecter of our faith, who for the joy set before Him endured the cross, despising the shame, and has sat down at the right hand of the throne of God (Hebrews 12:1-2).

Jesus had visions for going to the cross. How much more we need that vision for our liberating work. Vision makes men and women do heroic things. Vision comes from God's revelation to you of what your life can accomplish if you choose to *pour it out on someone else.* Jesus died for His children in obedience to His Father. God the Father showed Him what His death would accomplish. "Unless a grain of wheat falls into the earth and dies, it remains by itself alone; but if it does, it bears much fruit" (John 12:24). His death gave us life.

The cure for Christian loneliness is to be found in serving your

---

[2] 2 Timothy 3:13

brothers and your sisters, living to see that those who come behind you have more chance for freedom than you received. This kind of love is the core of life itself. As the Psalmist said, when "goodness and mercy follows us," we find ourselves in the house of the Lord forever.[3] A heart spent on others, opens heaven's doors.

It is commitment to make a difference that gives us the inner compulsion to bow our heads humbly under Jesus' yoke. That yoke spells death to comfort and privatized Christianity. It will carry you to people and sweat and sacrifice. It may carry you to other nations. It will permit neither quitting nor freely turning territory over to Christ's enemies.

But those who wear His yoke, upon entering into their final rest, receive the ultimate reward for their service: "Well done, good and faithful slave; you were faithful in a few things, I will put you in charge of many things. Enter into the joy of your Master" (Matthew 25:21). These burden-bearers have found the truth that it is the Savior, the people, and the principles you are committed to die for that give meaning to your life.

A Call To Clear Thinking

Right action begins with right thinking, and all right thinking begins by believing God's Word. In His Word, God says repeatedly that the nations belong to Jesus the King, and that men are simply acting in His stead until he returns. Biblical thinking must be your first prophetic act as you move against the world system. Right thinking will then lead you on to right speaking.

Speak and Pray Like a Liberating Steward

Godly speaking comes from three sources: the Holy Spirit, the Word, and human hearts aligned with both. Prayer is our most effective form of liberating speech. "I shall run the way of your commandments, for you will enlarge my heart" (Psalm 119:32).

Prayer is the act of aligning our hearts with God's heart. When we get close to Him He tells us what He cares about. He enlarges our hearts and makes us capable of feeling what He feels.

---

[3] Psalm 23

Christians need to pray each time they watch the evening news and read the daily newspaper. Out of our hearts must come the cry that will align their hearts with God's: "Father, what are You doing with this person or that situation? What are You after, and what can I do to help You put Your Word into action in this situation? How should I pray about this effectively and how can I get others to pray with me? What books should I be reading that will help prepare me for this issue? Where do You deal with these issues in Your Word?"

Christians must pray regularly that God will continually cleanse their minds from the false ideas and principles pressed on them by the world. We need to be "deprogrammed" from the continuous lies of the nations' jailer. His media attacks against both the imprisoned nations and the Liberators' minds never stop. Intercession both as individuals and in groups must break the spiritual and mental chains of deception before there is political action. It took God forty years with Moses in the wilderness to "deprogram" him from the lies of the Egyptian jailers before Moses was ready to go back and liberate God's people. Don't neglect prayer. And don't neglect your time in the desert.

Prayer was the political tool of Daniel[4] and Hezekiah.[5] It was what brought Saul of Tarsus down and changed him from the persecutor to the apostle.[6] It brought judgment through Samson.[7] It is and always will be our first line of attack and the only sure way to victory.

Prayer changes things. It redirects people and situations. Although it is the most powerful force on earth, it is probably the most under-used. Most Christians always pray "constructively," that is, they pray for good things to happen to specific people. We must continue fervently in this kind of prayer. However, in the political realm, much of our praying must be to remove before we build. Jeremiah, one of the more political of God's prophets, prayed in interdiction against the apostate kingdoms of his day. He was told by the Lord:

---

[4] Daniel 9:9-14   [5] Isaiah 37:16-20   [6] Acts 7:60   [7] Judges 16:28

See, I have appointed you this day over the nations and over the kingdoms, to pluck up and to break down, to destroy and to overthrow, to build and to plant (Jeremiah 1:10).

Liberators must begin to pray for removal, and in some cases, destruction of apostate systems. This kind of prayer is found throughout the scriptures. Psalm 83:15-18 is a classic example:

So pursue them with Thy tempest, and terrify them with Thy storm. Fill their faces with dishonor, that they may seek Thy name, O Lord. Let them be ashamed and dismayed forever; and let them be humiliated and perish, that they may know that Thou alone, whose name is the Lord, art the Most High over all the earth.

The key to this prayer is found in "that they may know that Thou alone, whose name is the Lord, art the Most High over all the earth." These are redemptive prayers for the opponents of God, if these opponents repent and are humbled.

Christians must stop being "nice" so that they can become redemptive. Through real and accurate assessments of the true needs of apostate people and ungodly situations, Christians can implore heaven's power to judge, correct, heal and rebuild. The keys to the kingdom of God upon the earth are in the Spirit-directed prayers of the saints.[8]

Liberators Must Do Their Homework

Study to show thyself approved unto God, a workman that needeth not to be ashamed, rightly dividing the word of truth (2 Timothy 2:15).

In order for Christians to bring more than simply loud noises and zeal into the political and social realm, they must acquire knowledge and biblical answers. It is mostly the secular thinkers who have studied the issues affecting the nations and who prescribe remedies to the nations' problems. To say, "The humanists' answers don't work," is not enough. The nations must have something to put into their place that *will work*. God doesn't

---

[8] Matthew 16:19

just want to restore souls, he intends to restore the whole environment of man's life back into his original plan: "And that He may
send Jesus, the Christ appointed for you, whom heaven must
receive until the period of restoration of all things...spoken by
the mouth of His holy prophets from ancient time" (Acts 3:20,
21). Restoration will necessitate that Christians know and are working toward what God intended in the first place to be going on
in every sphere of life.

Meaningful involvement always comes around to specializa-
tion. No one is an expert on everything. The issues confronting
the nations are vast and often complex. Most current problems
are "tied in knots" because the world is so lost and has been
operating out of confused and self-contradicting principles. We
must identify the biblical principles applicable to a particular situation This untying of complexities will require supernatural in-
sight mixed with plain old hard work and study.

Becoming a Liberator

How does one find what God wants him to become an expert
in amidst this jungle of social problems? The answer is really
quite simple, and it employs two biblical principles.

First, what issues have captured your heart? In Ephesians 3:1,
the Apostle Paul says, "For this reason I, Paul, the prisoner of
Christ Jesus for the sake of you Gentiles." Paul did what he did
because a *particular group of people* had captured his heart. In
his case it was the Gentiles (nations). If you will pray and watch
where your heart goes you will begin to discover the people and
issues that God has put on *your heart.*[9]

Second, God asked Moses in Exodus 4:2, "What is that in
your hand?" God always gives us clues as to where He wants
us to go by asking us to identify the resources we already have.
Do you have a trade, a skill, or a degree in a particular field?
What spiritual or political issues do you find yourself always going back to? These resources are a clue to what God wants you
to do. He plans our lives long before we discover what those plans

---

[9] Psalm 37:4

are. He prepared our resources long before most of us even notice them. Who is in your heart? What is in your hand? As you begin to answer these questions, you will find the purposes of minstry the Lord has given to you.

Liberators Must Unite

While one can put to flight a thousand, two can put to flight ten thousand (Deuteronomy 32:30).

Unity of purpose brings disproportionate power. Some of the following areas of concern speak to issues that currently imprison our nation. Many of these issues already have groups formed around them throughout the nation. You may want to work with one of these groups:[10]

1. Family and women's issues
2. Pro-life issues
3. Student mobilization
4. Foreign missions work with others who see the need to rebuild the nations
5. Economic, business and trade issues
6. Christian medicine and health care
7. Christian agriculture and land use
8. Christian education
9. Christian media and art
10. Christian candidate training and issues analysis
11. Christian foreign policy issues

Behind each of these doors and many others like them lie vast realms of consecrated life, freedom, and abundance for the Liberator who sells out to God. If you have the faith for involvement, the Spirit and Word have given you the liberating keys.

The Local Church Holds The Keys

Much of the Church today has communicated the four following erroneous messages, both to believers and unbelievers:

1. Full time ministry in the church is limited to either pastoral

---

[10] See Appendix A for additional information including how to locate activist organizations.

or evangelical work with all other Christian work secondary. You can be a teacher, but only to the extent that you teach other emerging church leaders how to pastor or evangelize.

2. If prophetic work (political involvement) was supposed to be something in which the Church was to be directly involved, it would be made a full time ministry like the pastor or the evangelist. At best, operating rescue missions and providing clothing for the poor fulfills the Church's social responsibilities. What God really meant when he said to disciple the nations was merely to evangelize them.

3. God is not interested in the structure of society. He is only interested in making sure all people have been evangelized and that those saved are pastored.

4. Religion is an issue of private conscience and should not be an issue of public debate.

This greatly restricted view of Christianity is the fruit of false pietism and confusion about the true nature of the gospel of the kingdom. The unsaved love this shrunken view of the Church's mission because it keeps the Church out of their way and gives them a monopoly on social rulership and the delineation of moral issues.

But none of these misconceptions is true. The local church needs to supply armies of men and women who are trained and support to change whole cultures. The Church's army needs more than chaplains.

We need local churches that are committed to bringing Christ to the nations as well as to the individual sinner. We need local churches that are committed to support Liberating Christians in their many endeavors to liberate the nation. We need local churches where financial support goes out to more than just those who pastor, administrate or teach. Commitment follows money and our church resources are being allocated far too narrowly.

We need to unlock the prophetic gifts in God's people by committing ourselves to investing in ministries that equip people to change society and minister to the spiritual and physical needs of men. We need business councils, city-wide prayer leaders, ministries that feed and house and vocationally train the needy.

In short, we need myriad thousands of churches that will take back the work of caring for the people from the secular government.

Do You Have A Hero's Heart?

For David, after he had served the purpose of God in his own generation, fell asleep, and was laid among his fathers (Acts 13:36).

The highest service that any man or woman can do is to serve the purposes of God in his own generation. The Liberator hungers to be relevant and to make a difference. He or she is not content simply to go to heaven. Each is inwardly desperate to see the law and love of heaven kiss the earth.

The Lord's prayer is frequently upon his lips when he rises and when he lies down at night. "Father what can I do to see your church spread the kingdom to the souls and institutions upon the earth more effectively?"

The Liberator knows that the battlefield is the mind; the territory to be won is the earth; and that which is to be discipled is God's political creation called the nations. The Liberator knows that every self-seeking reality must bow before Christ, be it the soul of a man or the soul of a nation. And he is giving himself to see that happen in the home, in the school, in the marketplace, and in the government.

Liberating Your Captives

Every good soldier wants to release his fellow soldiers who have been taken captive. Jesus was no different. He took His brethren back to His Father.[11] The Creator wants His whole earth released from the chains of sin that hold it in disobedience. The "Lord's Prayer" is the cry of our Savior for the wayward nations to come back to their Creator, through the Church that He has set upon the earth to tend and steward them. But the stewards have been foolish, giving back the earth to the enemies of our Father, forgetting that it was His. So the Father sent His only

[11] Ephesians 4:8

170

begotten Son and redeemed the world, and set His servants on His appointed land once again, after He had freed them from the consequence of their own disobedience.

Now, having our souls, he wants His earth and the nations He has placed upon it. He is waiting for us to do what our Savior did when He returned to God's presence. We, like Jesus, are to bring with us liberated men as we liberate the nations of God's world.

Look outward and see the captives. Now look inward and see the heart that the Liberator Himself has put within you.

And they overcame him because of the blood of the Lamb and because of the word of their testimony, and they did not love their life even to death (Revelation 12:11).

Anderson, Kerby, ed. **A Christian World View**. Grand Rapids, MI: Zondervan Publishing Company, 1984.

Bahnsen, Greg L. **By This Standard**. Tyler, TX: Institute for Christian Economics, 1985.

Booker, Christopher. **The Seventies: The Decade That Changed The Future**. Briarcliff Manor, NY: Stein & Day, 1980.

Chilton, David. **Productive Christians in an Age of Guilt-Manipulators**. Tyler, TX: Institute for Christian Economics, 1981 (Second edition, revised, July, 1982).

DeMar, Gary. **God and Government: A Biblical and Historical Study**. Atlanta, GA: American Vision Press, 1982.

Hall, Verna M, compiler. **Christian History of the Constitution of The United States of America: Christian Self-Government**. San Francisco, CA: Foundation for American Christian Education, 1961.

Johnson, Paul. **Modern Times: The World from the Twenties to the Eighties**. New York, NY: Harper and Row, 1983.

LaHaye, Tim. **The Battle for the Mind**. Old Tappan, NJ: Fleming H. Revell, 1980.

McMaster, Jr., R.E. **No Time For Slaves**. Phoenix, AZ: Reaper Publishing, 1986.

Naisbitt, John. **Megatrends**. Los Angeles, CA: Warner Books, 1982.

North, Gary. **Backward, Christian Soldiers? An Action Manual for Christian Reconstruction**. Tyler, TX: Institute for Christian Economics, 1984.

_____, ed. **Biblical Blueprint Series**. Fort Worth, TX: Dominion Press, 1986, 1987.

_____, ed. **Foundations of Christian Scholarship: Essays in the Van Til Perspective**. Vallecito, CA: Ross House Books, 1976.

Novak, Michael. **The Spirit of Democratic Capitalism**. New York, NY: Simon & Schuster, 1982.

Richardson, John R. **Christian Economics: The Christian Message to the Marketplace**. Houston, TX: St. Thomas Press, 1966.

Robertson, Pat. **The Secret Kingdom**. Nashville, TN: Thomas Nelson Publishers, 1982.

Rushdoony, Rousas John. **Christianity and The State**. Vallecito, CA: Ross House Books, 1986.

_____. **Institutes of Biblical Law**. Nutley, NJ: The Craig Press, 1973.

_____. **Salvation and Godly Rule**. Vallecito, CA:Ross House Books, 1983.

_____. **The Foundations of Social Order: Studies in the Creeds and Councils of the Early Church**. Tyler, TX: Thoburn Press, [1968] 1978.

_____. **The Nature of the American System**. Fairfax, VA: Thoburn Press, 1965, 1978.

_____. **The Politics of Guilt and Pity**. Fairfax, VA: Thoburn Press, 1978.

Schaeffer, Francis A. **A Christian Manifesto**. Westchester, IL: Crossway Books, 1981.

Schaeffer, Franky. **A Time for Anger: The Myth of Neutrality.** Westchester, IL: Good News Publishers, 1982.

Schlossberg, Herbert. **Idols for Destruction.** Nashville, TN: Thomas Nelson Publishers, 1983.

Simon, William. **A Time For Truth.** New York, NY: Readers Digest Press, 1978.

Skousen, W. Cleon. **The Making Of America: The Substance and Meaning of the Constitution.** Washington D.C.: The National Center for Constitutional Studies, 1985.

Slater, Rosalie J. **Teaching and Learning American Christian History: The Principle Approach.** San Francisco, CA: Foundation for American Christian Education, 1965.

Solzhenitzyn, Alexander. **Warning to the West.** Farrar & Strauss

——————. **Mortal Danger.** Harper and Row.

Sutton, Ray R. **That You May Prosper: Dominion By Covenant.** Tyler, TX: Institute for Christian Economics, 1987.

Whitehead, John W. **The Second American Revolution.** Elgin, IL: David C. Cook Publishing Company, 1982.

——————. **The Stealing of America.** Westchester, IL: Crossway Books, 1983

Old Testament

THE OLD TESTAMENT

31	108	49:22	153
31:23	108	58:12	119
Ecclesiastes:		60:1-3	131
4:12	35	60:1-41	39; 152
Isaiah:		61:1-4,6	112
1:22,23	100	*Jeremiah:*	
5:13	51	1:10	166
5:20	94	2:19	139
6:3	125	*Ezekiel:*	
9:6	131	47:9,10	143
9:6,7	83; 124	*Daniel:*	
9:7	18	2:21	85
10:1	19	4:31,32	124
20:4	108	9:9-14	165
26:9	139	10:13	35
33:22	86	*Haggai:*	
37:16-20	165	2:7-9	151
42:3,4	75	*Zechariah:*	
42:4	66	14:5-9	148
49:6	110		

THE NEW TESTAMENT

Matthew:		7:5	68
4:1-11	4	7:24-27	151
4:4	3; 26	9:10,11	138
4:19	135; 136	10:34	131
4:28-32	124	11:19	138
5:13	107	12:29	3
5:13-16	xvii; 107; 110	12:30	138
5:17-19	67	12:42-44	148
5:18,19	68	12:47-50	24
5:38-40	70	13:24-30	130
6:10	xiv; 66; 125	13:33	123
7:1,2	68	13:47,48	138
7:1-3	74	15:6	62

APPENDIX A

For additional information about the author, Dennis Peacocke, the Rebuilders Seminar Series, audio and video presentations and other resource materials, please write to the address below.

For additional copies of this book, please clip or photocopy the form below and send to:

Strategic Christian Services, 131 Stony Circle, Suite 750, Santa Rosa, California 95401.

☐   Please send me _____ copies of *Winning the*
        Battle For The Minds of Men
        @ \$9.00 per copy..........................\$ _____
        Please add \$2.00 per book
        shipping/handling ....\$ _____
        California residents add
        6% sales tax.............................\$ _____

☐   I would like to receive Dennis Peacocke's
        monthly newsletter **The Rebuilder** featuring
        his commentary, *The Bottom Line.*
        I enclose a \$15 minimum donation...........\$ _____

I enclose my check/money order payable to
Strategic Christian Services for a total of.............\$ _____

| Title | First Name | Last Name |

Address

City/State/Zip

183